Centre for Effective Altruism
Suite 2, Littlegate House
16-17 St Ebbes Street
Oxford
OX1 1PT
United Kingdom

www.80000hours.org

Printed in the United States by CreateSpace

First Printing, 2016

ISBN 1537324004
ISBN-13 978-1537324005

Copy editing and interior design by Peter Orr
Images by Maria Gutierrez (unless otherwise credited)

80,000 Hours

Find a fulfilling career
that does good

Benjamin Todd

and the 80,000 Hours team

About the authors

80,000 Hours is an independent non-profit organization founded in Oxford in 2011. It performs research into career choice, and provides online and in-person advice.

Benjamin Todd is the CEO and co-founder of 80,000 Hours. He grew the organization from a student society at Oxford to a non-profit that's raised $1.3m in donations, and has had one million readers. He has a Master's degree in Physics and Philosophy from Oxford, has published in climate physics, and speaks Chinese, badly.

Ben is advised by the rest of the 80,000 Hours team, including Professor Will MacAskill, author of Doing Good Better, co-founder of the Effective Altruism movement, and one of the youngest professors of philosophy in the world.

Contents

Introduction

You have about 80,000 hours in your career: 40 hours a week, 50 weeks a year, for 40 years. This means your choice of career is one of the most important decisions you'll ever make.

Make the right choices, and you can help solve some of the world's most pressing problems, as well as have a more rewarding, interesting life. But for such an important decision, there's surprisingly little good advice out there.

Back in 2011, we were at Oxford trying to work out what to do with our own careers. We wanted to find a job we'd enjoy that would also make the world a better place. We wondered: should we work at a non-profit, do graduate study, work in business and contribute through philanthropy, or something else entirely?

But we couldn't find much good advice. Most career advice was just about how to apply to different jobs, not how to decide what to do in the first place. And when it came to doing good with your career, the advice focused on things like social work, teaching, or working in CSR, and it didn't seem like these were obviously the best options. Most people we spoke to didn't even use career advice – they would just speak to friends and try to figure it out for themselves.

So we started doing our own research and presenting our findings. And to our surprise, people listened.

In November 2011 we founded 80,000 Hours in collaboration with academics at Oxford. In July 2012, we raised funding and hired a team. Since then we've spoken to hundreds of experts, read all the relevant literature we could find, and had over a million people read our online advice.

We're looking to provide the advice we wish we'd had – easy to use, transparently explained and based on the best evidence available. We're a non-profit supported by individual donations and we don't take money from recruiters or companies, so all our advice is impartial. Our only aim is to help you to have a greater positive impact with your career.

We still have a lot to learn, but we don't think there's any else who's done as much systematic research into this topic as us.

As of today, over a thousand people have significantly changed their career plans due to our advice (and they're just the ones we know about). Our readers have pledged over $30 million to effective charities and founded ten new organizations focused on doing good. Some are saving hundreds of lives in international development, some are working on neglected areas of government policy, and others are developing ground-breaking technology.

In this guide, we'll summarize all the key things we've learned so far.

If you could make your career just 1% higher impact, or 1% more enjoyable, it would be worth spending up to 1% of your career doing so. That's 800 hours – five months of full-time work. We're going to take little more than a weekend.

How to use this guide

Here's what we'll cover:

1. What makes for a dream job?
2. Can one person make a difference?
3. What are the world's most pressing problems?
4. In which career can you help the most people?
5. Which jobs put you in the best position for the future?
6. How to find the right career for you.
7. How to make your career plan.
8. How to find a job.
9. Why community is key.

The first four sections are about what options to aim for long-term. The rest is about how to get there and take action. So, we'll work from long-term issues towards short-term ones.

The guide is especially aimed at students and recent graduates in their 20s, but most sections are relevant to everyone. If you're midway through your career, focus on chapters one to four, six, seven and nine.

At the end, there are also a few more resources:

- A short summary of our key ideas.
- Some additional articles that further explain key ideas.
- Summaries of our top career reviews.
- Summaries of our problem area profiles.

To get the most out of this guide, we recommend reading each chapter, then doing the exercises that go with each one. The best thing to do is set aside a day or two to work through everything. At the end, use our online tool to check you've mastered all the ideas and make your new career plan:
http://80k.link/HWC

When we've delivered this content over an afternoon, often over half the people who attended changed what they had planned to do with their lives.

So let's get started. What's the best way you can use your 80,000 hours?

Benjamin Todd
CEO and Co-founder, 80,000 Hours

CHAPTER 1

What makes for a dream job?

BY THE FIFTH YEAR, JIM REALLY REGRETTED
FOLLOWING HIS CHILDHOOD PASSION FOR ICE CREAM...

We all want to find a dream job that's enjoyable and meaningful, but what does that actually mean?

Some people imagine that the answer involves discovering their *passion* through a flash of insight, while others think that the key elements of their dream job are that it be easy and highly paid.

We've reviewed two decades of research into the causes of a satisfying life and career, drawing on over 60 studies, and we didn't find much evidence for these views.

Instead, we found six key ingredients of a dream job. They don't include income, and they aren't as simple as "following your passion".

In fact, following your passion can lead you astray. Steve Jobs was passionate about Zen Buddhism before entering technology. Condoleezza Rice was a talented classical musician before she started studying politics.

Rather, you can develop passion while doing work that you will find enjoyable and meaningful. The key is to get good at something that helps other people.

(For a full survey of the evidence on job satisfaction, follow the link in the footnote.[1])

Where we go wrong

The usual way people try to work out their dream job is to *imagine* different jobs and think about how satisfying they seem. Or they think about times they've felt fulfilled in the past and self-reflect about what most matters to them.

If this were a normal career guide, we'd start by getting you to write out a list of what you most want from a job, like "working outdoors" and "working with ambitious people". The best-selling career advice book of all time, *What Color is Your Parachute*, recommends exactly this. The hope is that, deep down, people know what they really want.

However, research shows that although self-reflection is useful, it only goes so far.

You can probably think of times in your own life when you were excited about a holiday or party, but when it actually

---

[1] 80000hours.org/articles/job-satisfaction-research

happened, it was just okay. In the last few decades, research in psychology has shown that this is common: we're bad at predicting what will make us most happy, and we don't even realize how bad we are. You can find an excellent overview of this research in *Stumbling Upon Happiness*, by Harvard Professor Dan Gilbert.

It turns out we're even bad at remembering how satisfying different experiences were. One well-established mistake is that we tend to judge an experience mainly by its ending. If you missed your flight on the last day of an enjoyable holiday, you'll probably remember the holiday as bad. This means we can't just trust our intuitions and even memories. Rather, we need a more systematic way of working out which job is best for us.

> *The fact that we often judge the pleasure of an experience by its ending can cause us to make some curious choices.*
>
> – Professor Dan Gilbert, *Stumbling Upon Happiness*

The same research that proves how bad we are at self-reflection can help us make more informed choices. We now have two decades of research into positive psychology – the science of happiness – as well as decades of research into motivation and job satisfaction. We'll summarize the main lessons of this research and explain what it means for finding a fulfilling job.

Two overrated goals for a fulfilling career

People often imagine that a dream job is well paid and easy.

One of the leading job rankings in the US, provided by *Careercast*, rates jobs on the following criteria:[2]

- Is it highly paid?
- Is it going to be highly paid in the future?
- Is it stressful?
- Is the working environment unpleasant?

Based on this, the best job in 2015 was: actuary.[3] That is, someone who uses statistics to measure and manage risks, often in the insurance industry.

It's true that actuaries are more satisfied with their jobs than average, but they're not among the most satisfied.[4] Only 36% say their work is meaningful,[5] so being an actuary isn't a particularly fulfilling career.

---

[2] Their 2015 methodology can be found at careercast.com/jobs-rated/2015-jobs-rated-methodology.

[3] careercast.com/jobs-rated/best-jobs-2015

[4] A national survey by the UK's Cabinet Office in 2014 (published by the University of Kent) found actuaries ranked 64th out of 274 job titles, putting them in the top 23%. kent.ac.uk/careers/Choosing/happiest-careers.htm

[5] Payscale's surveys, which cover tens of thousands of workers, found only 36% of actuaries found their work meaningful. See payscale.com/data-packages/most-and-least-meaningful-jobs/full-list.

So the *Careercast* list isn't capturing everything. In fact, the evidence suggests that money and avoiding stress aren't that important.

Money makes you happier, but only a little

It's a cliché that "you can't buy happiness", but at the same time, financial security is among most people's top career priorities.[6] Moreover, when people are asked what would most improve the quality of their lives, the most common answer is more money.[7] What's going on here? Which side is right?

A lot of the research on this question is of remarkably low quality. But several recent major studies in economics offer more clarity. We reviewed[8] the best studies available, and the truth turns out to lie in the middle: money *does* make you happy, but only a little.

Here are the findings from a huge survey in the United States in 2010:

---

[6] Net Impact, What Workers Want in 2012 - See Figure 1.1. netimpact.org/sites/default/files/documents/what-workers-want-2012.pdf

[7] Judge, Timothy A., et al. "The relationship between pay and job satisfaction: A meta-analysis of the literature." Journal of Vocational Behaviour 77.2 (2010): 157-167.

[8] 80000hours.org/articles/money-and-happiness

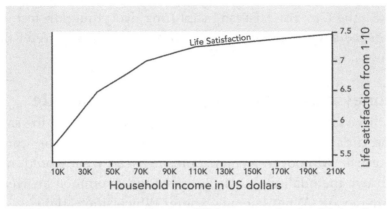

High income improves evaluation of life but not emotional well-being, D. Kahneman and A. Deaton, 2010.

People were asked to rate how satisfied they were with their lives on a scale from one to ten. The result is shown on the right, while the bottom shows their household income.

You can see that going from an income of $40,000 to $80,000 is only associated with an increase in life satisfaction from about 6.5 to 7 out of 10. That's a *lot* of extra income for a small increase.

But that's optimistic. If we look at day-to-day happiness, income is even less important. "Positive affect" is whether people reported feeling happy yesterday. The left shows the fraction of people who said "yes". This line goes flat at around $50,000, showing that beyond this point income had no relationship with day-to-day happiness.

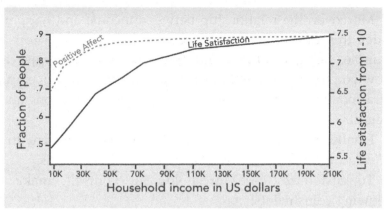

High income improves evaluation of life but not emotional well-being, D. Kahneman and A. Deaton, 2010.

The picture is similar if we look at the fraction who were "not blue" or "stress free" yesterday.

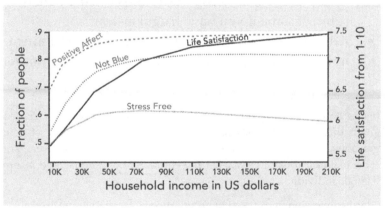

High income improves evaluation of life but not emotional well-being, D. Kahneman and A. Deaton, 2010.

These lines are completely flat by $75,000, so beyond this point, income had *no* relationship with how happy, sad or stressed people felt. This is hardly surprising – we all know people who've gone into high-earning jobs and ended up miserable.

Moreover, the relationship between income and happiness under this threshold may be caused by a third factor. For example, being healthy could both make you happier and allow you to earn more. If this is true, then the effect of earning extra money will be even weaker than the correlations above suggest.

Finally, $75,000 of household income is equivalent to an *individual* income of only $40,000 if you don't have kids.[9]

To customize these thresholds for yourself, make the following adjustments:

- Add $20,000 per dependent who does not work that you fully support.
- Add 50% if you live in an expensive city, or subtract 30% if you live somewhere cheap.
- Add more if you're especially motivated by money (or subtract some if you have frugal tastes).
- Add 15% in order to be able to save for retirement (or however much you personally need to save in order to

---

[9] This is based on the average household in the US having 2.5 people, although this is just an average across a wide range of family structures. Larger households enjoy 'economies of scale' by sharing houses, cars, and so on. This makes it tricky to say what the equivalent of a household income is for a single individual.

Standard conversion rates (used by international organizations) are:

- A single individual has an equivalence score of 1.
- A single extra adult adds another equivalence score of 0.5.
- Adding a young child to this adds an equivalence score of 0.3, while a teenager costs another 0.5.

Using this approximation means that a single individual requires about 53% as much as a typical household, averaged over their adult lives, to achieve the same standard of living.

be able to maintain the standard of living described above).

The average college graduate in the United States earns $68,000 per year over his or her life, while the average Ivy League graduate earns over $100,000.[10] The upshot is that if you're a college graduate in the US (or a similar country), you'll likely end up well into the range where more income has almost no effect on your happiness.[11]

Don't aim for low stress

Many people tell us they want to "find a job that's not too stressful." And it's true that in the past, doctors and psychologists believed that stress was always bad. However, we did a survey of the modern literature on stress, and today, the picture is a bit more complicated.

One puzzle is that studies of high-ranking government and military leaders found they had *lower* levels of stress hormones and less anxiety, despite sleeping fewer hours, managing more people and having greater demands placed on them.

One widely supported explanation is that having a greater sense of control – by setting their own schedules and determining how to tackle the challenges they face – protects them against the demands of the position.

There are other ways that a demanding job can be good or bad depending on context:

---

[10] Carnevale, Anthony P., Stephen J. Rose, and Ban Cheah. "The college payoff: Education, occupations, lifetime earnings." (2011).

[11] We have prepared a more thorough examination of the question of money and happiness at 80000hours.org/articles/money-and-happiness.

Variable		Good (or neutral)	Bad
Type of Stress	Intensity of demands	Challenging but achievable	Mismatched with ability (either too high or too low)
	Duration	Short-term	Ongoing
Context	Control	High control and autonomy	Low control and autonomy
	Power	High power	Low power
	Social Support	Good social Support	Social isolation
How to cope	Mindset	Reframe demands as opportunities (stress as useful)	View demands as threats (stress as harmful to health)
	Altruism	Performing altruistic acts	Focusing on yourself

This means the picture looks more like the following graph. Having a very undemanding job is bad – it's boring. Having demands that exceed your abilities is bad too: they cause harmful stress. The sweet spot is where the demands placed on you match your abilities – that's a fulfilling challenge.

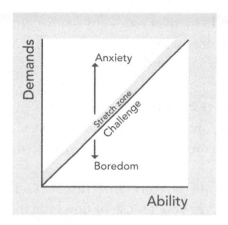

Instead of seeking to avoid stress, seek out a supportive context and meaningful work, and then challenge yourself.

What *should* you aim for in a dream job?

Professor Seligman, the founder of positive psychology, summarized the key ingredients of wellbeing as:

- Positive emotion – feeling happy day-to-day.
- Engagement – having challenging, absorbing tasks.
- Relationships – having supportive friends and family.
- Meaning – having a purpose higher than yourself.
- Achievement – being good at something.

We've applied these factors to our analysis of what to look for in a job – and combined them with research on job satisfaction and motivation – to come up with six key ingredients of a dream job.[12]

These are the six ingredients:

1. Work that's engaging

What really matters is not your salary, status, type of company and so on, but rather, what you do day-by-day, hour-by-hour.

Engaging work is work that draws you in, holds your attention, and gives you a sense of flow. It's the reason an hour spent editing a spreadsheet can feel like pure drudgery, while an hour playing a computer game can feel like no time at all: computer games are designed to be as engaging as possible.

What makes the difference? Why are computer games engaging while office admin isn't? Researchers have identified four factors:

- The **freedom** to decide how to perform your work.
- **Clear tasks**, with a clearly defined start and end.
- **Variety** in the types of task.
- **Feedback**, so you know how well you're doing.

Each of these factors has been shown to correlate with job satisfaction in a major meta-analysis (r=0.4), and they are widely thought by experts to be the most empirically verified predictors of job satisfaction.

That said, playing computer games is not the key to a fulfilling life (and not just because you won't get paid). That's because you also need...

---

[12] For our full examination of this topic, see 80000hours.org/articles/job-satisfaction-research.

2. Work that helps others

The following jobs have the four ingredients of engaging work that we discussed. But when asked, over 90% of people doing them say they don't find them meaningful:[13]

- Revenue analyst
- Fashion designer
- TV newscast director

These jobs, however, are seen as meaningful by almost everyone who does them:

- Fire service officer
- Nurse / midwife
- Neurosurgeon

The key difference is that the second set of jobs seem to *help other people*. That's why they're meaningful, and that's why helping others is our second factor.

There's a growing body of evidence that helping others is a key ingredient for life satisfaction. People who volunteer are less depressed and healthier. A randomized study showed that performing a random act of kindness makes the *giver* happier. And a global survey found that people who donate to charity

---

[13] Based on payscale.com surveys of over 2.7m Americans.

payscale.com/data-packages/most-and-least-meaningful-jobs/least-meaningful-jobs

payscale.com/data-packages/most-and-least-meaningful-jobs/most-meaningful-jobs

payscale.com/data-packages/most-and-least-meaningful-jobs/methodology

are as satisfied with their lives as those who earn twice as much.

None of these studies by themselves are decisive, but they form a body of evidence. Helping others isn't the only route to a meaningful career, but it's widely accepted by researchers that it's one of the most powerful.

(We'll explore jobs that really help people in the next chapter, including jobs that help indirectly as well as directly.)

3. Work you're good at

Being good at your work gives you a sense of achievement, one of the five ingredients of life satisfaction mentioned above.

It also gives you the power to negotiate for the other components of a fulfilling job, such as the ability to work on meaningful projects, undertake engaging tasks and earn fair pay. If people value your contribution, you can ask for these conditions in return.

For both reasons, skill ultimately trumps interest. Even if you love art, if you pursue it as a career but aren't good at it, you'll end up doing boring graphic design for companies you don't care about.

That's not to say you should only do work you're already good at. However, you at least have the *potential* to get good at it.

(In Chapter 6 we'll look in more detail at how to work out what you're good at.)

4. Work with supportive colleagues

Obviously, if you hate your colleagues and work for a boss from hell, you're not going to be satisfied.

Since good relationships are such an important part of having a fulfilling life, it's important to be able to become friends with at least a couple of people at work. And this probably means working with at least a few people who are similar to you.

However, you don't need to become friends with everyone, or even like all of your colleagues. Research shows that perhaps the most important factor is *whether you can get help* from your colleagues when you run into problems. A major meta-analysis found "social support" was among the top predictors of job satisfaction (r=0.56).

In fact, people who are disagreeable and different from yourself can be the people who'll give you the most useful feedback, provided they care about your interests. This is because they'll tell it like it is. In his book *Give and Take: A Revolutionary Approach to Success*, Professor Adam Grant calls these people "disagreeable givers".

When we think of dream jobs, we usually focus on the role. But *who* you work with is with is almost as important. A bad boss can ruin a dream position, while even boring work can be fun if done with a friend. So when selecting a job, will you be able to make friends with some people in the workplace? And more importantly, does the culture of the workplace make it easy to get help, get feedback and work together?

5. Lack of major negatives

To be satisfied, everything above is important. But you also need the *absence* of things that make work unpleasant. All of the following tend to be linked to job *dis*satisfaction.

- A long commute, especially if it's over an hour by bus.
- Very long hours.
- Pay you feel is unfair.
- Job insecurity.

Although these sound obvious, people often overlook them. The negative consequences of a long commute can be enough to outweigh many other positive factors.

6. Work that fits with the rest of your life

You don't *have* to get all the ingredients of a fulfilling life from your job. It's possible to find a job that pays the bills and excel in a side project; or to find a sense of meaning through philanthropy and volunteering; or to build great relationships outside of work.

We've advised plenty of people who have done this. There are famous examples too – Einstein had his most productive year in 1905, while working as a clerk at a patent office.

So this last factor is a reminder to consider how your career fits with the rest of your life.

Recap

Before we move on, here's a quick recap of the six ingredients. This is what to look for in a dream job:

1. Work you're good at,
2. Work that helps others,
3. Engaging work that lets you enter a state of flow (freedom, variety, clear tasks, feedback),
4. Supportive colleagues,
5. No major negatives like long hours or unfair pay, and
6. Work that fits your personal life.

Should you just follow your passion?

How can we sum this all up? "Follow your passion" has become a defining piece of career advice.

Source: Google Ngram

The idea is that the key to finding a great career is to identify your greatest interest – "your passion" – and pursue a career involving that interest. It's an attractive message: just commit to your passion, and you'll have a great career. And when we look at successful people, they *are* often passionate about what they do.

Now, we're fans of being passionate about your work. The research above shows that intrinsically motivating work makes people a lot happier than a big paycheck.

However, there are three ways "follow your passion" can be misleading advice.

One problem is that it suggests that passion is all you need. But even if you're interested in the work, if you lack the other six factors, you'll still be unsatisfied. If a basketball fan gets a job involving basketball, but works with people they hate, receives unfair pay, or finds the work meaningless, they are still going to dislike their job.

In fact, "following your passion" can make it harder to satisfy the six ingredients, because the areas you're passionate about are likely to be the most competitive, which makes it harder to find a good job.

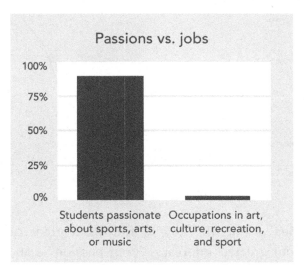

Source: University of Montreal[14] and Canadian Census Data

A second problem is that many people don't feel like they have a career-relevant passion. Telling them to "follow their passion" is no help. If you don't have a "passion", don't worry. You can still find work you'll become passionate about.

Others feel like they have many passions, and aren't sure which one to focus on. The six ingredients above, however, let you make finer-grained comparisons.

The third problem is that it can make people needlessly limit their options. If you're interested in literature, it's easy to

[14] Vallerand, Robert J "Les Passions de l'Âme: On Obsessive and Harmonious Passion" Journal of Personality and Social Psychology 2003, Vol. 85, No. 4, 756–767.

think you must become a writer to have a satisfying career, and ignore other options.

But in fact, you can start a career in a new area. If your work helps others, you practice to get good at it, you have engaging tasks, and you work with people you like, then you'll *become* passionate about it. The six ingredients are all about the context of the work, not the content. Ten years ago, we would *never* have imagined being passionate about giving career advice, but here we are.

Many successful people are passionate, but often their passion developed alongside their success, rather than coming first. Steve Jobs started out passionate about Zen Buddhism. He went into technology as a way to make some quick cash. But as he became successful, his passion grew, until he became the most famous advocate of "doing what you love".

Rather than having a single passion, in reality our interests change often, and more than we expect.[15] Think back to what you were most interested in five years ago, and you'll probably find that it's pretty different from what you're interested in today. And as we saw above, we're bad at knowing what really makes us happy.

This all means you have more options for a fulfilling career than you might first think.

---

[15]   See   80000hours.org/2015/02/we-change-more-than-we-expect-so-keep-your-options-open.

Do what contributes to the world

Rather than "follow your passion", our slogan for a fulfilling career is: get good at something that helps others. Or simply: *do what contributes*.

We highlight "getting good", because if you find something you're good at that others value, you'll have plenty of career opportunities, which gives you the best chance of finding a job with the other ingredients – engaging work, good colleagues, lack of major negatives, and fit with rest of life.

You can have all the other five ingredients, however, and still find your work meaningless. So you need to find a way to help others too.

If you put making a valuable contribution to the world first, you'll develop passion for what you do – you'll become more content, ambitious and motivated.

Example: Jess was interested in philosophy as an undergraduate, and considered pursuing a PhD. The problem was that although she finds philosophy interesting, it would have been hard to make a positive impact within it. Ultimately, she thinks this would have made it unfulfilling.

Instead, she switched into psychology and public policy, and is now one of the most motivated people we know.

To date, over 1,000 people have made major changes to their career path by following our career advice. Many switched into a field that didn't initially interest them, but that they believed was important for the world. After developing their skills, finding good people to work with, and the right role, they've become deeply satisfied.

Here are two more reasons to focus on getting good at something that helps others.

You'll be more successful

If you make it your mission to help others, then people will want to help you succeed.

This sounds obvious, and there's now empirical evidence to back it up. In the excellent book *Give and Take*, Professor Adam Grant argues that people with a "giving mindset" end up among the most successful. This is both because they get more help, and because they're more motivated by a sense of purpose.

One caveat is that givers also end up unsuccessful if they focus *too* much on others, and burn out. So you also need the other ingredients of job satisfaction we mentioned earlier.

It's the right thing to do

The idea that helping others is the key to being fulfilled is hardly a new one. It's a theme from most major moral and spiritual traditions:

> *Set your heart on doing good. Do it over and over again and you will be filled with joy.*
> – Buddha

> *A man's true wealth is the good he does in this world.*
> – Muhammad

> *Love your neighbor as you love yourself.*
> – Jesus Christ

> *Every man must decide whether he will walk in the*
> *light of creative altruism or in the darkness of*
> *destructive selfishness.*
> – Martin Luther King, Jr.

What's more, as we'll explain in the next section, as a college graduate in a developed country today, you have an enormous opportunity to help others through your career. Ultimately, this is the real reason to focus on helping others – the fact that it'll make you more personally fulfilled is just a bonus.

Conclusion

To have a dream job, don't worry too much about money and stress, and don't endlessly self-reflect to find your one true passion.

Rather, get good at something that helps others. It's best for you, and it's best for the world.

But which jobs help people? Can one person really make much difference? That's what we'll answer in the next chapter.

Apply this to your own career

These six ingredients, especially helping others and getting good at your job, can act as guiding lights – they're what to aim to find a dream job long-term.

Here are some exercises to help you start applying them.

1. Practice using the six ingredients to make some comparisons. Pick two career options you're interested in, then score them from one to five on each factor.

2. The six ingredients we list are only a starting point. There may be other factors that are especially important to you, so we also recommend doing the following exercises. They're not perfect – as we saw earlier, our memories of what we've found fulfilling can be unreliable – but completely ignoring your past experience isn't wise either.

   - When have you been most fulfilled in the past? What did these times have in common?
   - Imagine you just found out you're going to die in ten years. What would you spend your time doing?
   - Can you make any of our six factors more specific? E.g. what *kinds* of people do you

most like to work with?

These questions should give you hints about what you find most fulfilling.

3. Now, combine our list with your own thoughts to determine the four to eight factors that are most important to you in a dream job.

4. When you're comparing your options in the future, you can use this list of factors to work out which is best. Don't expect to find an option that's best on every dimension, rather, focus on finding the option that's best on balance.

The bottom line: what makes for a dream job?

To find a dream job, look for:

1. Work you're good at,

2. Work that helps others,

3. Supportive conditions: engaging work that lets you enter a state of flow; supportive colleagues; lack of major negatives like unfair pay; and work that fits your personal life.

CHAPTER 2

Can one person make a difference? What the evidence says.

In the last chapter, we showed that getting good at something that helps others is the key to a fulfilling career, but what can you really do to help others?

Sometimes it feels like individuals can't do much, and that charity is ineffective. And that's often true.

A popular way to raise money for charity in the UK is sponsored skydiving. Every year, thousands of people gather donations for good causes and then throw themselves out of planes. This may sound like a win-win scenario: the fundraiser gets an exhilarating once-in-a-lifetime experience, and at the same time raises money for a good cause. What could be the harm in that?

A study of two popular parachuting centers found that over five years (1991 to 1995), approximately 1,500 people went skydiving for charity.[16] Collectively they raised more than

---

[16] Lee, C.T. et al. "Parachuting for charity: is it worth the money?" Injury, Int. J. Care Injured 30 (1999) 283-287, available at https://drive.google.com/file/d/0B4kMPIEI5Mb8NHdKT19Wc012aFE/view

£120,000, which seems pretty impressive. But the whole venture was badly misguided.

First, the cost of diving came out of the sponsored donations: of the £120,000 raised, only £45,000 ultimately went to the charities.

Second, the skydivers were mostly first-time jumpers. The result? They had 163 injuries, and the average hospital stay was nine days.

The cost of all these injuries to the UK's National Health Service was around £610,000. That means that every £1 raised for the charities, which ironically were mostly health-related, cost the NHS about £13.

But this doesn't mean all efforts to do good fail. In fact, some people's careers have had a huge impact, and there's a lot that *any* college graduate can do.

Some careers have more impact than others

How much good does a doctor do?

When people think of careers that make a difference, they tend to imagine jobs like teaching, social work and medicine. So, when we started 80,000 Hours, one of the first questions we asked was: how much good do these careers actually do?

We started by making estimates of the impact you'd have by becoming a doctor who practices clinical medicine. The main purpose of doctors is to improve health, so we tried to estimate how much extra "health" a doctor adds.

Working with a Cambridge public health researcher, Dr. Greg Lewis, we found that on average in the course of their career, a doctor in the UK will enable people to live an extra

120 years of healthy life, either by extending their lifespan or by improving their quality of health. There's a huge amount of uncertainty in this figure, but it's unlikely to be more than ten times higher. This research is due to be published and can be found in the footnotes.[17]

Using a standard conversion rate (used by the World Bank among others) of 30 extra years of healthy life to one "life saved", 120 years of healthy life is equivalent to four lives saved. There's no doubting that this is a significant impact, however it's less impact than many people expect doctors to have. There are three main reasons for this.

1. It's widely accepted by researchers that medicine has only increased average life expectancy by a few years. Most of the increase in life expectancy that's occurred in the last 100 years is instead due to better nutrition, better sanitation, higher wealth, and other factors besides medicine.

2. Doctors are only one part of the medical system, which also relies on nurses, hospital staff, and all the buildings and equipment. The impact of medical interventions is shared between all of these elements.

3. Most importantly, there are already many doctors in the developed world, so the most impactful procedures are going to get done whether or not you become a doctor. *Additional* doctors therefore only enable us to carry out procedures that deliver smaller and less certain health benefits.

---

[17] See 80000hours.org/career-reviews/medical-careers.

You can see this in the chart below, which compares different countries. On the side is the level of ill health in the population, measured in "DALYs" per 100,000 people, where one DALY is a year of life lost due to ill health. On the bottom is the number of doctors per 100,000 people.

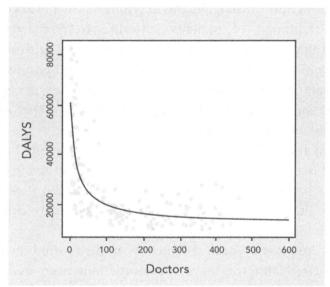

WHO data from 2004 (or latest available year). DALYs per 100,000 versus doctors per 100 000. Line is the best fitting hyperbola determined by non-linear least square regression.

You can see that the curve goes nearly flat once you have more than 150 doctors per 100,000 people. After this point (which is met by almost all developed countries), additional doctors only have a small impact.

So if you become a doctor, your career will probably have more impact than an ordinary job, but it will still not be a huge impact.

Who has had more impact? Examples from medical research

Despite this, some doctors have *much* more positive impact than the average.

In 1968, while working in a refugee camp on the border of Bangladesh and Burma, Dr. David Nalin made a breakthrough in the treatment of patients suffering from diarrhea. He realized that if patients were given water mixed with the right concentration of salt and sugar, they could be rehydrated at the same rate as they lost water. This prevents death from dehydration much more cheaply than with the existing treatment, an intravenous drip.

Since then, this astonishingly simple treatment has been used all over the world. The annual rate of child deaths due to diarrhea has fallen from 5 million to 1.3 million. Researchers estimate that in total about 50 million lives, mostly children's, have been saved due to the therapy.

This treatment would still have been discovered eventually even if Dr. Nalin was never involved. However, even if we suppose that he sped up roll-out of the treatment by only six months, the impact of Dr. Nalin's work would be to save about 500,000 lives.

This means that his impact was some 100,000 times greater than that of an ordinary doctor:

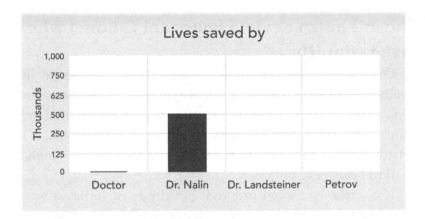

But Dr. Nalin is far from the most extreme example. Even just within medical research, there have been more impactful discoveries. Karl Landsteiner's discovery of blood groups likely saved tens of millions of lives.

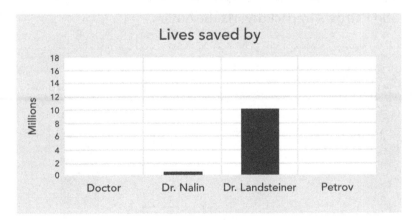

Thinking more broadly, Roger Bacon and Galileo pioneered the scientific method, without which none of these discoveries would have been possible (along with the industrial revolution and much more). You could make a good case for their work having a far greater impact still

The unknown Soviet Lieutenant Colonel who saved your life

Or consider the story of Stanislav Petrov. He was on duty in a Soviet missile base in 1983, when early warning systems apparently detected an incoming missile strike from the United States. The clear protocol was to order a return strike, but Petrov reasoned that the number of missiles was too small, so he didn't push the button.

If a strike had been ordered, hundreds of millions would have died, and it may have triggered all out nuclear war, leading to billions of deaths and, in the worst case, the end of civilization. Perhaps we could quantify his impact as saving one billion lives, and that's probably an underestimate because a nuclear war would have devastated scientific, artistic, economic and all other forms of progress.

So Petrov's impact dwarfs the others.

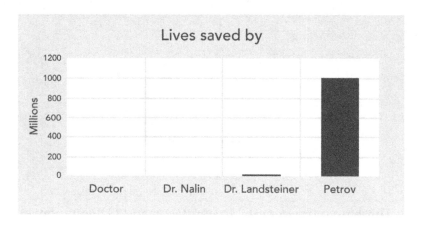

What does this mean for your career?

Some careers have huge positive effects, and some vastly more than others.

Some of this is due to luck – these people were in the right place at the right time. But it wasn't all luck: Landsteiner and

Nalin chose to use their intelligence to work on some of the most harmful health problems of their day, and it was also entirely foreseeable that someone high up in the Soviet military could have a large impact on the world by preventing conflict.

Since there are such big differences in impact between careers, if there's anything you can do to increase the chances of your career being among the high impact ones, it would really be worth doing. And we're going to show that you can do plenty.

These examples also show that the highest-impact paths might not be the most obvious ones, or traditional "do-gooder" paths. Being a doctor turned out worse than it first looks. And while being an officer in the Soviet military might not sound like a good thing to do with your life, Petrov probably did more good than our most celebrated leaders.

So how much impact can *you* have if you try? First, we'll give a conservative estimate: it turns out that *any* college graduate in the developed world can have a very substantial social impact in any career – perhaps even more than you could by becoming a doctor. Then we'll explore ways to do even more good by changing career.

But first, let's clarify what we mean by "making a difference". We've been talking about lives saved so far, but that's not all that matters.

What do we mean by "making a difference"?

When people talk about "positive impact", "the good you do" or the "difference you make", what does it actually mean?

Ultimately this is a philosophical question, but here's our answer: *social impact*. We define it as:

> *The number of people whose lives you improve, and how much you improve them.*

This means that there are two ways you can have more social impact: helping more people, or helping the same number of people to a greater extent (pictured below).

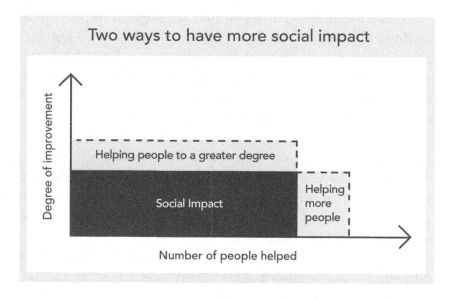

We chose this definition because it's broad enough to include a lot of things, but narrow enough that almost everyone agrees it's important.

There are a few more points to make about this definition before we go on.

1. Although we talked in the previous section about saving lives, social impact is *not* confined to this: improvements to quality of life can be just as

significant. That could involve making people happier, helping them reach their potential, or making their lives more meaningful.

2. We are usually uncertain about the social impact different actions will have, but that's okay, because you can use probabilities to make the comparison. For instance, a 90% chance of helping 100 people is roughly equivalent to a 100% chance of helping 90 people.

3. Your social impact includes all of the people your actions help, both immediately and over the coming decades and beyond. As a result, it may be better to seek an indirect impact. For example, if you improve the quality of government decision-making, that could have a huge social impact in the long run even if it doesn't help people right now. We'll come back to this in the next chapter.

4. Environmental impact is also included, but indirectly. If the environment degrades, then we and other animals will have worse lives, and eventually face extinction.

(There's more information about ways of making a difference in Appendix 1.)

How to make a big difference in any career

In our research, we've discovered that any college graduate in the developed world can have a significant social impact with little personal sacrifice, and without changing job.

Here's one way:

1. Take whatever job you find most personally fulfilling.
2. Give 10% of your income to the world's poorest people.

Today, you can give to the world's poorest people through GiveDirectly (givedirectly.org), a charity that provides one-off cash transfers to the poorest people in East Africa via mobile phone.

This isn't necessarily the best you can do. Rather, it's an option open to almost anyone that already does a lot of good.

How much good will this do?

As we saw in the last chapter, money goes further the less you have. We saw that in the US a doubling of income is associated with about half a point gain in life satisfaction, on a scale of one to ten.

Other surveys have found similar results across the world. This study covered over 160 countries, and here's a sample of the results:

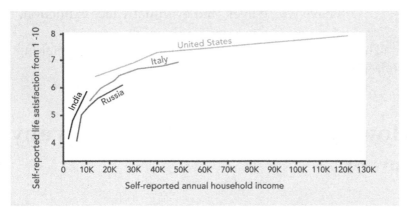

Stevenson, Betsey, and Justin Wolfers, *Subjective well-being and income: Is there any evidence of satiation?* No. w18992. National Bureau of Economic Research, 2013.

The poor in Kenya have an average individual income of about $200 per year, while the average US college graduate has an annual individual income of about $68,000. This means your money will go about 340 times as far if given to the Kenyan rather than spent on yourself.

If someone earning that average level of income were to donate 10%, it would be enough to double the annual income of 34 people living in extreme poverty each year, likely having a major positive impact on hundreds of people over your career.

In human terms: Grace, 48, is a typical recipient. She's a widow who lives with four children:

> I would like to use part of the money to build a new house since my house is in a very bad condition. Secondly, I would wish to pay fees for my son to go to a technical institute....
>
> My proudest achievement is that I have managed to educate my son in secondary school.
>
> My biggest hardship in life is [that I] lack a proper source of income.
>
> My current goals are to build and own a pit latrine and dig a borehole since getting water is a very big problem.

GiveDirectly has done a randomized controlled trial of their program, which found significant reductions in hunger, stress and other bad outcomes for years after the transfers are made. This trial adds to an already substantial literature on cash transfers, showing significant benefits.[18]

Most of the money is invested in assets, such as metal roofs and water equipment. The recipients spend the money on whatever they most need, rather than what external aid agencies think they need. Since the program requires little infrastructure, little money is lost on overhead.

How much sacrifice will this involve?

In this path, you get to do whatever job you find most personally fulfilling, which is much easier than switching jobs.

Moreover, you'll only give up 10% of your income. Normally when we think of doing good with our careers, we think of paths like becoming a teacher or charity worker, which can easily involve earning 50% less than you would in the private sector.

Finally, as we saw in the last chapter, extra income over $40,000 doesn't have that much effect on your happiness, while giving to charity probably makes you happier.

To take just one example from the literature, it was found that in 122 of 136 countries, if you answered "yes" to the question "did you donate to charity last month?", your life satisfaction was higher by an amount associated with a *doubling* of income. So we think there's a good chance that giving 10% makes you happier overall.[19]

---

[18] Full details of the evidence for the effectiveness of cash transfers can be found at givewell.org/International/top-charities/give-directly.

[19] See https://www.givingwhatwecan.org/sites/givingwhatwecan.org/files/attachments/giving-without-sacrifice.pdf

Higher impact than being a doctor

If you think there are charities that are more effective than GiveDirectly, then this path becomes even better.

The leading, independent charity evaluator, GiveWell, estimates that donations to Against Malaria Foundation save a life for about $3,000, as well as many other benefits in terms of quality of life and income.[20] This means that your donations could save more than two lives every year. This is such a good opportunity that even the most prominent aid skeptics don't challenge its worth.[21]

Earlier, we estimated that by becoming a doctor, you could save four lives over an entire career. Through donating to Against Malaria Foundation, you can match this impact in just two years. For this reason, many of the doctors we've advised have decided to focus on having an impact through research, public health, or donating, rather than directly through treating patients.

If you think opportunities *even* better than Against Malaria Foundation exist (as in fact we do[22]), then giving 10% is even better again. This might mean funding "high risk" options like policy advocacy or research.

In fact, if everyone in the richest 10% of the world's population gave 10% to whichever problems they think are most pressing, that would be $7 trillion per year. Just 2% of that would be enough to raise everyone in the world above the $1.25/day poverty line by simply giving them cash. We could

---

[20] See givewell.org/international/top-charities/amf for more details.

[21] See blog.givewell.org/2015/11/06/the-lack-of-controversy-over-well-targeted-aid.

[22] See 80000hours.org/articles/best-charity.

then provide universal education, double all scientific research spending, start a manned mission to Mars, fund a new renaissance in the arts...and still have more left over.

How is this possible?

It's astonishing that we can do so much good with so little sacrifice. Why is this possible?

Consider one of the most important graphs in economics: the graph of world income:

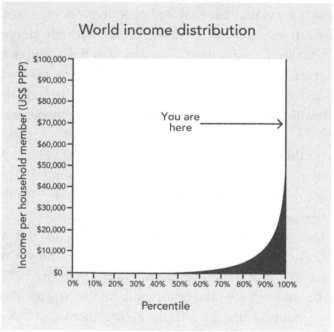

Source: *Doing Good Better*, by Will MacAskill, 2015.

The bottom shows the percentage of people with each level of income. Income has been adjusted for how much it will buy in a person's home country (i.e. purchasing power parity). If the world were completely equal, it would be a horizontal line.

We know we're rich, but we don't think of ourselves as the richest people in the world – we're not the bankers, CEOs or celebrities. But actually, if you earn $53,000 per year and don't have kids, then globally speaking, *you are the 1%*.

As we saw, the average US college graduate will earn $68,000 over their lives, so if you're reading this, you will probably be somewhere in that big spike on the right of the graph (and perhaps even way off the chart), while almost everyone else in the world is in the flat bit at the bottom that you can hardly even see.

There's no reason to be embarrassed by this fact, but it does mean that it's important to consider how you can use your good fortune to help those without your advantages. In a more equal world, we could all just focus on helping those around us, and making our own lives go well. But it turns out we have an enormous opportunity to help other people with little cost to ourselves – and it would be a terrible shame to waste that.

Take action right now

All of us at 80,000 Hours were so persuaded by these arguments that we pledged to give at least 10% of our lifetime income to effective charities. We did it through an organization called Giving What We Can, who we're partnered with. Our co-founder, Will, actually went a bit further and pledged to give all his income above $35,000 to charity.

Giving What We Can enables you to take a public pledge to give 10% of your income to the charities you believe are most effective. They also provide research-backed recommendations on where to give.

You can take the pledge in just a few minutes. It's likely to be the most significant thing you can do right now to do more good with your life.

It's not legally binding, you can choose where the money goes, and if you're a student, it only commits you to give 1%. You'll be joining over 2,000 people who've collectively pledged over half a billion dollars.

And if you're not quite ready yet, Giving What We Can allows you to pledge 2% for one year, to see how it goes before making any long-term commitment.

Take the pledge here:

http://80k.link/GWC

What if you don't want to give money?

Just as we happen to be rich by virtue of where we were born, we also happen to have political influence for the same reason.

Rich countries have a disproportionate impact on issues like global trade, migration, climate change and technology policy, and are at least partly democratic. So rather than giving money, you can advocate for important issues.

It might seem like you can't have any real influence through political advocacy, but that turns out to be wrong.

Let's take perhaps the simplest example: voting in elections. Several studies have used statistical models to estimate the chances of a single vote determining the US presidential election.[23] If you live in a state that's strongly in favor of one candidate, then it's almost zero. But if you live in a

---

[23] See 80000hours.org/2016/11/why-the-hour-you-spend-voting-is-the-most-socially-impactful-of-all.

state that's contested, it's between one in ten million and one in one million. That's quite a bit higher than winning the lottery.

And remember, the US Federal Government is big. Really big. Let's imagine one candidate wanted to spend 0.2% more of GDP on foreign aid. That would be about $320bn extra foreign aid over their four year term. A 1 in 10 million chance of that is $32,000 dollars.

The figures are similar in other rich countries - smaller countries have less at stake, but each vote counts for more.

So voting could be the most important hour you'll spend that year.

Alternatively, let's suppose you don't have any money or influence yourself. Well, at the very least, you probably know someone who does. So you can make a difference by helping or influencing them.

For instance, we know someone who set up 1% payroll giving at their company, and by doing that, raised far more money for charity than they could have given themselves.

Or consider Kyle. He became the assistant to a scientist he thinks is doing world-changing work. If he can save that scientist time then he's equally enabling more research to get done.

You don't need to throw yourself out of a plane to do good. Due to our fortunate positions, there's a lot we can do to effectively make a difference without making significant sacrifices, whatever jobs we end up in. We've covered three examples:

- Giving 10% to the world's poorest people
- Using our political influence, such as by voting.
- Supporting others in having an impact.

Which careers are fulfilling and high-impact?

What about if you're willing to change job too? If you can make such a big difference in all of these simple ways, it starts to suggest what directing your career towards social impact could achieve. That's what we'll cover next.

The bottom line: can one person make a difference?

- Some careers have far more impact than others, so it's worth thinking about what you could achieve.
- Any college graduate in the developed world can make a major difference to the lives of hundreds of people. They can do this by donating 10% of their income to the world's poorest people.
- They can also contribute by using political influence, such as by voting, or supporting others in doing good.

CHAPTER 3

What are the world's most pressing problems?

What can you do to increase the chance that your career will be successful and really help people?

An obvious place to start is to think about which problems in the world are in most need of attention – education, climate change, poverty – then work out what you could do about them.

But, if you ask people "what global problem should I focus on?" they'll ask in return "what are you interested in?"

Your motivation is important, but you might happen to be interested in a problem that's really hard to solve, that already has a lot of attention, or that's just not very important, and so end up having much less impact than you could.

In this chapter, we'll explain how to avoid these mistakes and pick the right problem. We're going to introduce a four-part framework for comparing global problems, then at the end we'll apply it to work out which problems are most pressing. We developed the problem framework with help from the Global Priorities Project, a research group at Oxford, and using work by the Open Philanthropy Project, a multi-billion dollar foundation.[24]

1. Work on problems that are neglected

Most people end up working on whichever social problem first grabs their attention. That's exactly what our co-founder, Ben, did. Aged 19, Ben was most interested in climate change. However, this wasn't the result of a careful comparison of the pros and cons of different areas. Rather, by his own admission, he'd happened to read about it, and found it engaging because it was sciency and he was geeky.

The problem with this is that you're far more likely to stumble across the problems that are most widely discussed. And if they're widely discussed, then they probably also already have a lot of people working on them.

All else equal, the more effort that's already going into a problem, the harder it is for *you* to be successful in that area and make a meaningful contribution. This is due to *diminishing returns* – people take the best opportunities first, so once a lot of resources have gone into a problem, it becomes harder and harder to make a difference, like this:

---

[24] See more detail on the framework at 80000hours.org/articles/problem-framework.

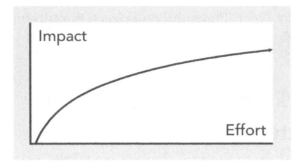

This means that the problems you'll happen to stumble across are probably *not* going to be the highest impact ones.

Instead, seek out problems that are unfairly neglected by others. The more neglected the problem, the more chance there is of finding *low-hanging fruit*: great opportunities to have a social impact that haven't already been taken, and won't be quickly taken by someone else.

In the previous chapter, we saw that medicine in the UK is a relatively crowded problem – there are already plenty of doctors and health spending is high, which makes it harder for you to make a big contribution. Health in poor countries, however, receives much less attention, and that's one reason why it's possible to save a life for only about $3,000.

Putting this factor into practice means looking for something that other people are systematically missing. Perhaps the victims aren't in a position to speak for themselves, or it's happening a long way away, or affects our grandchildren rather than us. This is harder than it looks, because it means going against the crowd.

2. Work on problems with the largest scale

We tend to assess the importance of different social problems using our intuition. However, our intuition is bad at grasping large differences in scale.

For instance, one study found that people were willing to pay about the same amount to save 2,000 birds from oil spills as they were to save 200,000 birds, even though the latter is objectively one hundred times better. This is an example of a common error called scope neglect.

Or consider this BBC article (emphasis mine):

> *The nuclear power stations will all be switched off in a few years. How can we keep Britain's lights on?*
> *...unplug your mobile-phone charger when it's not in use.*

This so annoyed David MacKay, a Physics professor at Cambridge, that he decided to find out exactly how bad leaving your mobile phone plugged in really is. He plugged a charger into a watt-meter to measure the power it uses. No reading. He plugged in two chargers. No reading. Finally, having plugged in six chargers, he registered a reading of 0.1 Watts.[25]

The bottom line is that even if *no mobile phone charger were ever left plugged in again*, Britain would save at most *0.01%* of its personal power usage (and that's leaving aside industrial usage

---

[25] See the story of his attempt to find out here:
www.inference.eng.cam.ac.uk/sustainable/charger.

and the like). So even if entirely successful, a quick estimate shows this BBC campaign could have no noticeable effect. MacKay said it was like "trying to bail out the Titanic with a tea strainer".

Instead that effort could have been used to change behavior in a way that could have 1,000 times as large an impact, such as installing home insulation.

So which problems have the greatest scale? In the previous chapter, we said that social impact depends on the extent to which you help others live better lives. So based on this, a problem has greater scale (i) the larger the number of people affected, (ii) the larger the size of the effects per person and (iii) the larger the long-run benefits of solving the problem.

Scale is important because the effect of activities on a problem is often proportional to the size of the problem. Launch a campaign that ends 10% of the phone charger problem, and you achieve very little. Launch a campaign that persuades 10% of people to install home insulation, and it's a much bigger deal.

3. Work on problems that are solvable

This also sounds obvious, but in practice, people often work on interventions without any evidence that they are actually doing any good.

Here's an example in the field of reducing youth crime. Scared Straight takes kids who have committed misdemeanors to visit prisons and meet convicted criminals and confront their likely future if they don't change their ways. The concept proved popular not just as a social program but as entertainment; it was adapted for both an acclaimed documentary and a TV show on A&E, which broke ratings records for the network upon its premiere.

There's just one problem with Scared Straight: it has been proven to cause young people to commit *more* crimes. The effect is so significant that the Washington State Institute for Public Policy estimated that each $1 spent on Scared Straight programs causes more than $200 worth of social harm.[26]

Some attempts to do good, like Scared Straight, make things worse. Many more fail to have an impact. David Anderson of the Coalition for Evidence Based Policy estimates:

> *Of (social programs) that have been rigorously evaluated, most (perhaps 75% or more), including those backed by expert opinion and less-rigorous studies, turn out to produce small or no effects, and, in some cases negative effects.*

This suggests that if you chose a random government or charity program to get involved in, there's a decent chance that *you'll have no impact at all.*

Worse, it's very hard to tell which programs are going to be effective ahead of time. Don't believe us? Try our ten question game at 80000hours.org/articles/can-you-guess/, and see if you can guess what's effective. The game asks you to guess which social interventions work and which don't. We've tested it on hundreds of people, and they don't do better than chance.

---

[26] Petrosino, Anthony et al. "Scared Straight and other juvenile awareness programs for preventing juvenile delinquency: A systematic review of the randomized experimental evidence." The Annals of the American Academy of Political and Social Science 589.1 (2003): 41-62.

So, before you choose a social problem, ask yourself two questions: (i) Is there an intervention to make progress on this problem with rigorous evidence behind it? (ii) If not, can you test new interventions, in order to learn about what works? If the answer to both of these is no, then it's probably best to find something else, unless the problem is exceptionally big and neglected.

4. Your personal fit

If you're going to be much more motivated to work on one problem rather than another, that's important too. We recommend using your motivation as a tiebreaker between the most pressing problems. We'll discuss how to assess personal fit in chapter 6.

If you already have in-depth expertise that's especially relevant to one kind of problem, that's also important. If you're early in your career, however, then you can develop your expertise in a more useful direction.

Now let's apply the framework.

Example: Developing-world poverty vs. US poverty

When we think of making a difference, the first thing that comes to mind is often doing good in our local communities, usually in rich countries like the US and UK. In fact, in the US, only 4% of charitable donations are spent on international causes.[27]

However, if you apply the framework, it's clearly more pressing to help the poor in developing countries.

Factor	US poverty	Developing-world poverty
Scale	46.5m people living on less than $11,000 per year.	1.2 billion people living on less than $500 per year (PPP adjusted).
Neglectedness	$900 billion of welfare payments.	$134 billion of all foreign aid.
Solvability	Most US social interventions don't work, and we mostly don't know which (as we saw above).	Cash transfers work (as we saw in the last chapter) and there are even better interventions within global health.

Global poverty is more pressing on each of the three dimensions. (See references in footnotes.[28])

---

[27] In 2014, $15 billion out of $358 billion. See https://givingusa.org/giving-usa-2015-press-release-giving-usa-americans-donated-an-estimated-358-38-billion-to-charity-in-2014-highest-total-in-reports-60-year-history.

[28] **Number of Americans in poverty**

The key reason developing-world poverty is more pressing is that the global poor have far fewer resources than the poor in the US. In fact, the poor in the US have about 22 times as much income per capita as the global poor, and that's adjusted for the fact that money goes further in poor countries (PPP adjusted). As we saw in the previous chapter, this means each unit of resources given to them will go much, much further.

The US census report "Income and Poverty in United States: 2014" finds 46.7m Americans living below the US poverty line.

Foreign Aid spending

Official Development Assistance data finds total spending of $134,838 million in 2013. There is also international philanthropy, but we don't think adding it would more than double the figure. The US is the largest source of philanthropic funding at $300-400bn, but only a couple of percent goes to international causes. A Giving US report estimated that US giving to "international affairs" was only $15bn in 2014. Moreover, if we were to include international philanthropy, we'd need to include philanthropic spending on the poor in the US.

US welfare

Estimates of welfare spending vary depending on exactly what is included. Total spending also varies from year to year. We used a representative figure from a Forbes article (forbes.com/sites/peterferrara/2011/04/22/americas-ever-expanding-welfare-empire): "The best estimate of the cost of the 185 federal means-tested welfare programs for 2010 for the federal government alone is nearly $700 billion, up a third since 2008, according to the Heritage Foundation. Counting state spending, total welfare spending for 2010 reached nearly $900 billion, up nearly a fourth since 2008 (24.3%)."

Number of global poor

A World Bank report, "The State of the Poor", found that 1.2bn people were living below $1.25 per day (purchasing power parity adjusted) in 2010. This is equivalent to $460 per year.

This suggests if faced with the choice of working at a charity that helps those in the US or the poor in Africa, you'll have a greater impact by focusing on the global poor.

This isn't to deny there's a great deal of suffering caused by poverty in rich countries. Rather, it's to say you *can do more to help* if you focus on global poverty rather than rich country poverty. You only have 80,000 hours in your career, so you have to make tough choices about where to focus.

Why is this important?

We made a quantitative version of the problem framework and have applied it to some of the most pressing problems we've found so far. We're reviewing more problems all the time.

Intuitively, you might think if you rated problems on how pressing they are, and put them on a graph, you'd end up with something like this. Some problems are more pressing than others, but most are pretty good.

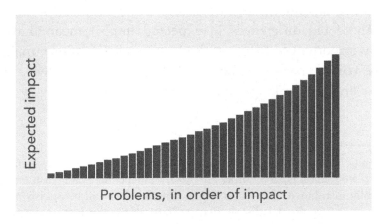

But instead we find that it looks more like this – some problems are *far* more pressing than others.

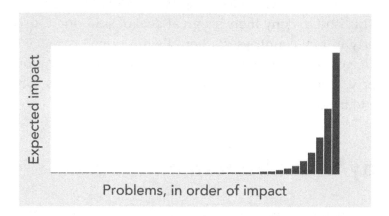

In fact, that's exactly what we should expect. The problems vary on all three factors in our framework, and the factors multiply together. A problem that scores highly based on all three factors will come out way ahead of the rest.[29]

You may remember that this graph has the same shape as the lives saved graphs we saw in the previous chapter. In fact, we find this shape shows up everywhere, making it one of our key ideas: *the most effective actions achieve far more than average.*

These big differences in expected impact mean that it's really important to focus on the best areas. Of course, making these comparisons is really hard, but if we don't, we could easily end up working on something with comparatively little

---

[29] If the effectiveness of a problem is the product of each of these factors (which we think it is), the factors are mostly independent, and each factor is normally distributed, then the combined distribution will be approximately log-normal. Log-normal distribution is "fat-tailed", which means that the more extreme values are much greater than the median.

impact. This is why many of our readers have changed which problem they work on.

Example: Niel Bowerman did years of climate advocacy when he was a student, and studied a PhD in climate physics to become a better advocate. At one point, he was even the climate science adviser to the office of the President of the Maldives. However, when he saw the evidence that he could have a greater impact by working on global health, he left climate advocacy behind, and helped to turn Giving What We Can into a full-time organization.

More recently, he decided that global catastrophic risks are even more important. Now, he's the manager of a world-leading research institute in this area (the Future of Humanity Institute). Each change took serious effort, but if changing area can enable you to have many times as much impact, and be more successful, then it's worth it.

So, which global problems are most pressing?

As we saw above, work that benefits the poorest people in the world has the potential to be highly effective, and likely far higher impact than work that only helps the poor in rich countries.

However, by thinking more broadly, we can find even bigger problems that few people are talking about. Based on our research so far, here's a list of problem areas, ranked on a combination of their scale, neglectedness, and solvability.

You can see more information about each in Appendix 9, or in the full profiles on our website (80000hours.org/problem-profiles/).

- Risks from artificial intelligence
- Promoting effective altruism
- Global priorities research
- Factory farming
- Biosecurity
- Nuclear security
- Climate change (extreme risks)
- Land use reform
- Smoking in the developing world
- Developing-world health

See our most up-to-date evaluation at 80000hours.org/articles/cause-selection.

Any ranking of problems is going to depend on difficult judgment calls, so different people will come to different conclusions. That's why we also created this quiz. It asks you a few questions, then uses your answers to adjust your ranking:

http://80k.link/QRT

Apply this to your own career

1. Using the resources above, write down the three global problems that you think are most pressing for you to work on.

2. Then visit our website and find our full problem profiles: 80000hours.org/problem-profiles. At the end of each profile, you can find a list of high-impact career options within that area. Note down any options that might be a good fit for you. Don't be too selective – the aim is just to come up with ideas for long-term options.

3. After you have your own list of problems, the next step is to work out how to help solve those problems. That's what we'll cover in the next part.

The bottom line: what are the world's most pressing problems?

The most pressing problems are most likely to have the following qualities:

Big in scale: What's the magnitude of this problem? How much does it affect people's lives today? How much effect will solving it have in the long run?

Neglected: How many people and resources are already dedicated to tackling this problem? How well allocated are the resources that are currently being dedicated to the problem? Are there good reasons markets or governments aren't already making progress on this problem?

Solvable: How easy would it be to make progress on this problem? Do interventions already exist to solve this problem effectively, and how strong is the evidence behind those interventions? Could you test a new intervention?

Personal fit: Could you become motivated to work on this problem? If you're later in your career, do you have relevant expertise?

You can find summaries of our evaluations of different problems areas in Appendix 9. To see our complete and up-to-date evaluations of problem areas, see:

http://80k.link/VEK

CHAPTER 4

In which career can you help the most people? Why the ideas you've heard for doing good with your career aren't the best.

Cartoon from SMBC.

Many people think of Superman as a hero. But he may be the greatest example of underutilized talent in all of fiction. It was a huge blunder to spend his life fighting crime one case at a time; if he'd thought a little more creatively, he could have done far more good. How about delivering vaccines to everyone in the world at super-speed? That would have eradicated most infectious disease, saving hundreds of millions of lives.

Here we'll argue that many people who want to make a difference with their career fall into the same trap as Superman. Graduates imagine becoming doctors or teachers – careers that help people directly. But these may not be the best fit for their particular skills. And like Superman fighting crime, these paths can often only help a limited number of people at once. Nobel Prize winner Karl Landsteiner discovered blood groups, enabling hundreds of millions of life-saving operations. He would have never been able to carry out that many surgeries himself.

At the same time, many graduates feel unfulfilled in their careers because they don't have a job that directly helps people. But there's no need for this. It can be fulfilling to help indirectly as well, so by being more open-minded and creative about how to do good, more people can find a career that both uses their unique skills and helps others.

Below we'll introduce four ways to use your career to contribute to solving the social problems you want to help work on (which we identified in the previous chapter). The four ways are earning to give, advocacy, and research, as well as direct work. We'll make concrete recommendations on how to pursue each approach.

You want to find options that both make a big contribution and are a good fit for you personally. Overall, the more pressing the problem, the larger your contribution and the better your personal fit, the more impact you'll have. There's no point pursuing a "high-impact" path if you'd be terrible at it. Later in the guide, we'll help you work out which of the options we cover is the best fit for you.

For now, just try to expand your options. The more options you consider, the easier to find a career that's both enjoyable and has a big positive impact on the world.

Approach 1: Earning to give

Would Bill Gates have done more good if he'd worked at a small non-profit? We don't normally think of software engineering as a path to doing good, but Gates has saved the lives of millions of children by funding vaccines. That's a huge amount of good, even if you're not keen on Microsoft.

We often meet people who are interested in a higher-earning job, like software engineering, but are worried they won't make a difference. Part of the reason is that we don't usually think of earning more money as a path for people who want to do good. However, there are many effective organizations that have no problem finding enthusiastic staff, but don't have the funds to hire. People who are a good fit for a higher-earning option can donate to these organizations, and make a large contribution indirectly.

Earning to give is not only for people who want to work in high-paying industries. Anyone who aims to earn more in order to give more is on this path.

Consider the story of Julia and Jeff, a couple from Boston with two children. Julia switched from non-profit admin work to social work at a prison. Jeff used to work as a research technician. He decided to train up to become a software engineer, and eventually got a job at Google. The couple were able to earn more than twice as much, so started to donate about half their income to charity each year.

By doing this, they probably have had more impact than they could by working directly in a non-profit. Compare Jeff's impact to that of the CEO of a non-profit:

	Google software engineer	Non-profit CEO
Salary	$250,000	$65,000
Donations	$125,000	$0
Money to live on	$125,000	$65,000
Direct impact of work	Positive	Very positive

Jeff can live on about two times as much as he would have earned in the non-profit sector, and still donate enough to fund the salaries of about two non-profit CEOs. On top of this, he may also have some positive direct impact too, since Google has developed valuable innovations like Google Maps and Gmail; *and* he thinks he's happier in his work because he enjoys engineering.

Moreover, Jeff and Julia can switch their donations to whichever organizations are most in need of funds at any given time, whereas it's harder to change where you work. This flexibility is particularly valuable because we don't know which problems will be most pressing in the future (see Chapter 5).

This opportunity exists because, as we covered in Chapter 2, we happen to live in a world with huge income inequality – it's possible to earn several times as much as a teacher or non-profit worker, and vastly more than the world's poorest people. At the same time, hardly anyone donates more than a few percent of their income, so *if you are* willing to do so, you can have an amazing impact in a very wide range of jobs.

We saw that any college graduate in a developed country can have a major impact by giving 10% to an effective charity. The average graduate earns $68,000 per year over their life, and 10% of that could save almost 100 lives if given to the Against Malaria Foundation for example.

If you could just earn 10% more, and donate the extra, then that's twice as much impact again. And if you think there are better organizations to fund than Against Malaria Foundation – perhaps working on different problems, or research or advocacy – the impact is even higher.

Since we introduced the concept of "earning to give" in 2011, hundreds of people have taken it up and stuck with it. Most give around 30% of their income, and some more than 50%. Collectively, they'll donate tens of millions of dollars to high impact charities in the coming years. In doing so, they are funding passionate people who want to contribute directly, but who otherwise wouldn't have the resources.

One of the people we advised in 2011, Matt, has donated over $1m while still in his 20s, and was featured in the New York Times. He finds his job more enjoyable too.

Another quit his job as a software engineer and founded a startup. He has pledged all of his income above minimum wage to charity. If his startup's current valuation is accurate, then he'll give millions of dollars to charity in the next decade. His startup also reduces paperwork for doctors, and so it has direct impact too.

Should you earn to give?

Earning to give has been our most memorable and controversial idea, attracting media coverage in the BBC, Washington Post, Daily Mail and many other outlets.[30]

For this reason, many people think it's our top recommendation. But it's not: it depends on your situation.

We think earning to give is an option worth considering when:

- **You're a good fit for a higher-earning option.** Don't become a software engineer if you'd hate it – you'll be more likely to burn out and put your career in a worse long-term position, and you won't earn that much anyway.

- **You want to gain skills in a higher-earning option** (for use in more direct work later on), and earning to give could help you to stay engaged with social impact while you do so. (In the next chapter we'll explain why it's important to gain "career capital".)

- **You're very uncertain about which problems are most pressing.** Earning to give provides the most flexibility because you can easily change where you donate, or even save the money and give later.

---

[30] bbc.co.uk/news/education-15820786

washingtonpost.com/news/wonk/wp/2013/05/31/join-wall-street-save-the-world

dailymail.co.uk/news/article-2334682/Young-professionals-joining-Wall-Street-save-world.html

Common objections to earning to give

- **Can people actually stick with it?** Won't they end up being influenced by their peers to spend the money on luxuries rather than donating? We were worried this would happen when we first introduced the idea, but it hasn't. Hundreds of people are pursuing earning to give and while some have left because they thought they could do more good elsewhere, no-one we know has simply given up their plans to donate. In part, this is because many people pursuing earning to give made public pledges of their intentions to donate, often through Giving What We Can (givingwhatwecan.org). The existence of a community that earns to give also makes it much easier to stick with today.

- **Don't many high-earning jobs cause harm?** We don't recommend taking a job that does a lot of harm in order to donate the money. In practice, most people who earn to give work in the fields of technology, asset management, medicine or consulting, and we think these positions do a small amount of good, or are neutral. Of course, there are some people who cause harm in these industries, but that's true of any industry.

  More broadly, there are lots of ways to earn more money, and we doubt all of these are harmful. There is also the option to make the industry better from the inside. If you're socially motivated and you replace someone who doesn't care about the harm they do, that may well be better for the world.

- **What if I wouldn't be motivated doing a high-earning job?** In that case, don't do one. We only recommend earning to give if it's a good fit. Just bear in mind, as we covered in Chapter 1, that you can become interested in more jobs than you might think.

- **Couldn't I have more impact doing something else?** There's a good chance that you could, as we'll cover in the rest of this chapter.

What's the best way to earn to give?

If you're already pretty certain that earning to give is not for you, then feel free to skip forward to "Approach 2 – Advocacy".

If you think you might be interested, here's a list of some of the best options we've found so far. You can find more detail on each option in Appendix 8.

These two paths are among the highest-earning and build your skills, although they are very competitive.

- Tech startup founder
- Quantitative trading

Some other promising options taken by plenty of people we've advised include:

- Management consulting
- Startup early employee
- Software engineering
- Data science

In all of these, you could earn far more than the average for a college graduate, while also putting your career in a better position for the future.

Law, investment banking and medicine are other obvious high-earning options, but we think they're a bit worse than the ones above based on their weaker combination of flexibility, growth of the area and direct impact.

We also think the following have promise and are a little easier to enter:

- Marketing
- Actuarial science
- Executive search
- Nursing

If you don't have a college degree, programming or sales can be good options. Some trades are also highly paid. For instance, the top 10% of plumbers earn over $89,000 per year, more than what the average college graduate earns.

There are many paths we haven't reviewed yet. Someone can earn to give in any career so long as they're earning more than they would have otherwise in order to donate more. Remember the example of Julia working as a social worker.

As a final note, some companies are willing to match charitable donations 1:1, or even more. By choosing an employer that does this, you may be able to double your donations with no effort.[31]

Which charities are most effective?

Many social interventions have no proven impact (as we saw in the previous chapter), and many other charities are poorly run black boxes. So, if you give to the wrong organization, you won't achieve much.

---

[31] 80000hours.org/2013/05/how-to-double-your-donations-with-no-extra-effort

On the other hand, so long as there's *at least* one highly effective organization to fund, then earning to give is high impact. You don't even need to limit yourself to funding charities – you could fund research, political advocacy or for-good for-profits instead.

When working out where to donate, a good starting point is GiveWell's top recommended charities.[32] GiveWell is the leading non-profit evaluator in the US and does a huge amount of research to find highly effective organizations. They currently recommended Against Malaria Foundation, which we mentioned earlier.

If you're giving a large amount of money, or don't want to focus on international development, then it can be worth doing your own research. Choose which problem areas you want to focus on (as we covered in the previous chapter), then find the best organizations within those areas, and give to those that have the greatest need for more funding. You can read more about where to donate at 80000hours.org/articles/best-charity.

Approach 2: Advocacy

One alternative to earning to give is advocacy – the promotion of solutions to pressing problems. Advocacy can also be pursued in a wide range of careers, and can be even higher impact than earning to give.

Consider the following options:

1.   Earn to give yourself.

---

[32] givewell.org/charities/top-charities

2. Earn to give yourself, and persuade a friend to earn to give as well.

The second path does more good – in fact probably about twice as much – and this illustrates the power of advocacy.

Many of the highest impact people in history have been advocates of one kind or another. Take Rosa Parks, who refused to give up her seat to a white man on a bus, sparking a protest which led to a Supreme Court ruling that segregated buses were unconstitutional. Now, Parks was a seamstress in her day job, but in her spare time she was very involved with the civil rights movement. After she was arrested, she and the NAACP worked hard and worked strategically, staying up all night creating thousands of fliers to launch a total boycott of buses in a city of 40,000 African Americans, whilst simultaneously pushing forward with legal action. This led to major progress for civil rights.

There are many examples you don't hear about, like Viktor Zhdanov, who was one of the highest impact people of the twentieth century.

In the twentieth century, smallpox killed around 400 million people, far more than died in *all* wars and political famines. Credit for the elimination often goes to D.A. Henderson, who was in charge of the World Health Organization's elimination program. However, the program already existed before he was brought on board. In fact, he initially turned down the job. The program would probably have eventually succeeded even if Henderson hadn't accepted the position.

Zhdanov single-handedly lobbied the WHO to start the elimination campaign in the first place. Without his involvement, it would not have happened until much later, and possibly not at all.

So why has advocacy been so effective in the past?

First, ideas can spread quickly, so advocacy is a way for a small group of people to have a large effect on a problem. A small team can launch a social movement, lobby a government, start a campaign that influences public opinion, or just persuade their friends to take up a cause. In each case, they can have a lasting impact on the problem that goes far beyond what they could achieve directly.

Second, advocacy is neglected. This is because there's usually no commercial incentive to spread socially important ideas. Instead, advocacy is mainly pursued by the small number of people willing to dedicate their careers to making the world a better place.

Advocacy is also neglected because it's uncomfortable to stand up to the status quo, and it's often difficult to see the effect of your efforts, which makes it less motivating than doing good directly. Zhdanov was more important to the elimination effort than Henderson, but Henderson got the credit. For these reasons, advocacy can be a high impact path for those who *are* willing to step up.

In fact, there's reason to think advocacy is typically better than earning to give. One reason is that everyone wants more money so there's a lot of competition, which places a limit on how much you can easily earn (and subsequently donate). There's a lot less competition to spread good ideas, for the reasons we just discussed. So we expect that it would be possible for many people to influence more money than they could donate.

Advocacy is also an area where the most successful efforts do *far* more than the typical efforts in the field. The most successful advocates influence millions of people, while others might struggle to persuade more than a few friends. This means if you're a good fit for advocacy, it's often the best thing you can do, and you're likely to achieve far more by doing it yourself than you could by funding someone to engage in advocacy on your behalf.

What's the best way to become an advocate?

If you're already pretty certain that advocacy is not for you, then feel free to skip forward to "Approach 3: Research".

As with giving money, you can advocate for solutions to pressing problems in *any* job.

To do that, go over the problems you think are most pressing (from the last chapter) and then look for small behaviors or ideas you could promote that would make a difference if they spread, like voting in an election or giving to a certain charity. Often it's best to lead by example, helping to set expectations, rather than being pushy.

Taking a stable job and doing advocacy part-time can be effective because you don't need to worry about funding your advocacy, which helps you to stay independent and take bigger risks. You'll also be seen as more impartial.

Finally, you'll be in a better position to advocate for attention to pressing problems if you're successful in your field, because you'll be more credible and make more influential connections. So sometimes the best path for advocacy is just to enter the field where you have the greatest chances of success. We'll discuss how to do this in Chapter 6.

But what about if you want to focus more directly on advocacy? Here are some options that are promising if you're a good fit, placed roughly in order of influence. Full profiles are included towards the end of this book. Could any be a good fit for you?

1. Political and policy positions

Like it or not, politicians have a huge influence. At the same time, relatively few people try to become or advise politicians, which means each person involved potentially has a large influence (quantitative estimates can be found at 80000hours .org/career-reviews/party-politics-uk). So, we need the most able and altruistic people possible in these positions.

For these reasons, if party politics is a serious option for you, and you're a good fit, then it's likely to be the most influential path. Also bear in mind that, if you don't want to be on the front lines yourself, there are plenty of advisory positions that can be highly influential, such as being a staffer or researcher, or working elsewhere in a political party.

There are also other promising policy positions that offer influence and political networks:

- Working in government, especially if you can get into more prestigious positions (e.g. the Civil Service Fast Stream in the UK), or positions especially relevant to the problems you think are most pressing (e.g. in the aid department if you're focused on international development or defense if you're focused on bio-security).
- "Influencer" positions, such as think tank research and lobbyists.

Just bear in mind that if you promote worse policies than would have been promoted otherwise, you could do a large amount of harm instead of good. The more influence you have, the larger the upside *and* downside. So, it's only a good idea to seek political positions if you have good reason to expect you'll be better at the job, or promote neglected policies.

Example: Owen was doing research in pure math, which he thought would have little impact. Instead he transferred into global priorities research, a small, new field that needs people with good analytic skills. He became the first employee of the Global Priorities Project, which advises policymakers about which global problems are most pressing, and which has already advised high levels of the UK government.

2. Positions with a public platform

Some jobs let you reach a large number of people, such as:

- **Journalism.** A typical article at a major media company has 10,000 to 100,000 views, so there's a lot of scope to reach people with new ideas. Vox.com regularly writes about Game of Thrones to drive traffic, but they also write articles about effective philanthropy. Last year, they were responsible for almost 10,000 views to GiveWell's site, already bringing them 200 new donors who have collectively donated over $100,000. Journalists can also build good networks.

- **Public intellectual.** If you can get an academic position, then you could focus your time on advocacy rather than research. Due to the status given to academics at top universities, it's relatively easy to build a following and get media attention.

- **Positions in the media.** Pursuing fame in arts and entertainment is another option, but we don't usually recommend it because the odds of success are extremely low. However, we expect there are other positions in the media that are promising, such as working in TV producing news, documentaries and comedy that draw attention to important issues.

3. Managers and grant-makers at influential organizations

Some jobs give you a say over large budgets. These jobs are often unglamorous and not widely known compared to their influence.

One path we've reviewed is being a grant-maker in a large charitable foundation (such as the Gates Foundation). Program officers usually oversee budgets of about $10 million per year. If you could introduce new ways to spend this money slightly more effectively, it could easily have a greater impact than earning to give or working directly.

We think these paths might also fall into this category, but we haven't reviewed them in depth yet:

- Program manager in international organizations.
- Science grant-makers.
- Government grant-makers.

4. Professional positions that let you meet lots of influential people

We've reviewed:

- Tech startup founder.
- Management consulting.
- Founding an international development non-profit (and other effective non-profits).

These positions can also make it easier to do advocacy on the side, though it's not the main reason to take them.

Law, finance and medicine also fit into this category, but have some downsides compared to consulting, which we cover in the next chapter. Similarly, there are professional services and executive search, which are less competitive, but also less prestigious than consulting.

There are probably more good paths in this category which we haven't reviewed yet, like being a philanthropic adviser or a teacher of talented students.

Approach 3: Research

People often pan academics as ivory tower intellectuals whose writing has no impact. And we agree there are many problems with academia that mean researchers achieve less than they could. However, we still think research is often high impact, both within academia and outside.

Along with advocates, many of the highest impact people in history have been researchers. Consider Alan Turing. He was a mathematician who developed code breaking machines that allowed the Allies to be far more effective against Nazi U-boats in WW2. Some historians estimate this enabled D-day to happen a year earlier than it would have otherwise. Since WW2 resulted in 10 million deaths per year, Turing may have saved about 10 million lives.

And he invented the computer.

Turing's example shows that research can both be theoretical and high impact. Much of his work concerned the abstract mathematics of computing, which wasn't initially practically relevant, but became important over time.

On the applied side, we saw lots of examples of high impact medical research in Chapter 2.

Of course, not everyone will be an Alan Turing, and not every discovery gets adopted. Nevertheless, we think research *on average* is effective, and frequently better than working directly on a problem. Why?

First, when new ideas are discovered they can be spread incredibly cheaply, so it's a way that a single career can change a field. Moreover, new ideas accumulate over time, so research contributes to a significant fraction of long-run progress.

However, only a relatively small fraction of people are engaged in research. Only 0.1% of the population are academics,[33] and the proportion was much smaller throughout history. If a small number of people account for a large fraction of progress, then on *average* each person's efforts are significant.

Second, this is exactly what we'd expect from economic theory. Most researchers don't get rich, even if their discoveries are extremely valuable. Turing made no money from the discovery of the computer, whereas today it's a multibillion dollar industry. This is because the benefits of research come a long time in the future, and can't usually be protected by patents. This means there's little commercial incentive to do research relative to its importance. So if you *do* care more about social impact than profit, then it's a good opportunity.

In fact, the more fundamental the research, the harder it is to commercialize, so, all else equal, we'd expect fundamental research to be more neglected than applied research, and therefore higher impact. Unfortunately, people who want to have an impact often focus on more applied issues rather than

[33] See www.richardprice.io/post/12855561694/the-number-of-academics-and-graduate-students-in

fundamental ones. (Though bear in mind that applied issues are often more *urgent* than fundamental ones.)

Like advocacy, research is especially promising when you're a good fit, because the best researchers achieve much more than the median. Most papers only have 1 citation, whereas the top 0.1% of papers have over 1,000 citations. And when we did a case study on biomedical research, remarks like this were typical:

> *One good person can cover the ground of five, and I'm not exaggerating.*

If you might be a top 10% researcher in a pressing problem area, then it's likely to be the highest impact path for you.

What research areas are high impact?

For our full guide to doing high-impact research, both within and outside academia, see Appendix 5.

Example: Hauke became unsatisfied with his potential for impact in academia during a neuroscience PhD. He applied to almost all our top recommended career paths, and was offered a position by Giving What We Can. He now leads their efforts to research the cost-effectiveness of different charities.

Don't forget supporting positions

Becoming an academic administrator doesn't sound like a high impact career, but that's exactly why it is. Research requires administrators, managers, grant-makers, and communicators to make progress. Many of these roles require very able people who understand the research, but because they're not glamorous or highly paid, it can be hard to attract the right people. For this reason, if a role like this *is* a good fit for you, then it can be promising. What ultimately matters is not who does the research, but that it *gets done.*

A hero of ours is Seán Ó hÉigeartaigh. He studied for a PhD in comparative genomics, but ultimately decided to pursue academic project management. He became manager at the Future of Humanity Institute, which undertakes neglected research into emerging catastrophic risks, like engineered pandemics. He did a heroic amount of work behind the scenes to keep things running as funding rapidly grew. When there was an opportunity to start a new group in Cambridge, he used what he'd learned to lead efforts there too – at one point managing both groups. The field would have moved much more slowly without his management.

If you're interested in these positions, the best path is usually to pursue a PhD, pick a field, then apply to research groups.

Approach 4: Direct work

If you *do* want to help directly, how can you do that most effectively?

The problem with many direct work positions is that they're not neglected. For instance, in Chapter 2, we saw that clinical doctors in rich countries don't usually have a large impact because there are already many doctors in these countries, so the most important and impactful procedures are going to get done anyway. In Chapter 3, we saw that most social interventions in rich countries don't have any proven effects. It's more effective to focus on an approach that's more neglected.

Another problem is that many want to work at organizations that are more constrained by funding than by the number of people enthusiastic to work there. This means if you don't take the job, it would be easy to find someone else who's almost as good. Think of a lawyer who volunteers at a soup kitchen. It may be motivating for them, but it's hardly the most effective thing they could do. Donating one or two hours of salary could pay for several better-trained people to do the work instead. Or they could do pro bono legal work, and contribute in a way that makes use of their valuable skills.

Other direct work positions limit your potential influence. Think of Superman fighting criminals one by one.

However, there are plenty of other situations when working directly is the most effective thing to do. There are many great teams working on innovative, neglected solutions to pressing problems. If you're a good fit for one of these, and they're finding it hard to hire (they are "talent-constrained"), then it can be the best option.

Example: Maria is a graphic designer from Costa Rica who went to art school in New York. She considered earning to give, but instead decided to move back to Costa Rica to cut down her costs, and do freelance work for charities she thinks are high-impact and need her skills.

If an effective organization doesn't exist within the area, then you could help found one. This was our thinking with

80,000 Hours: we knew no-one else was systematically doing this research.

Here's another area where this might be true. As of the last decade, several very large foundations have been created that want to fund charities that carry out evidence-based health interventions, such as the Gates Foundation, CIFF, and the Open Philanthropy Project (which is partnered with GiveWell). However, these foundations are short of projects that meet their criteria. If you could build expertise in getting health interventions efficiently implemented, you could raise tens of millions in funding from these foundations, and have far more impact than earning to give.

This is what Joey and Kate are doing. They left college early to focus on fundraising for charities like Against Malaria Foundation. However, they realized it would be even higher impact to try to set up something new. They spent six months reviewing a list of health interventions, and found one that looked effective, was simple to roll out, but didn't have a charity focusing on it.

They settled on text reminders for vaccinations in India, which have been shown in four randomized controlled trials to make it significantly more likely for people to get vaccinated. They're now setting up this organization and already have raised $200,000 from the Open Philanthropy Project.

However, you don't need to be the leader of an organization. As with research management, operations roles are both vital and difficult, but because these positions are unglamorous, it's often hard to attract the right people.

Finally, direct work can be for-profit as well as non-profit. For instance, Send Wave enables African migrant workers to transfer money to their families through a mobile app for fees of 3%, rather than 10% fees with Western Union. So for every $1 of revenue they make, they make some of the poorest people in the world several dollars richer. They've already had an impact equivalent to donating millions of dollars, and they're growing fast. The total size of the market is hundreds of billions of dollars, and several times larger than all aid spending. If they can slightly accelerate the roll out of cheaper ways to transfer money, it'll have a big impact.

If you're providing a service directly to beneficiaries, a for-profit can be more effective because you get better feedback on whether your service is useful, and you can scale up more quickly. Non-profits are best when they're doing something that's very hard to commercialize, such as research, advocacy, and the provision of public goods like a clean environment, or services like education that take a long time to pay off.

However, sometimes it's even possible to use for-profits to do socially important research and provide public goods. Elon Musk's Tesla sells fancy electric cars to rich people, which isn't very high impact. But the real mission of the company is to develop cheaper batteries that will make it much easier to transition to a green economy, and eventually electrify all of transport. Musk also created SpaceX, which makes money by selling cheap rockets to NASA, but the real mission of the company is to speed up the colonization of space, and make humanity more likely to survive a disaster on Earth.

How can you find a good direct work position?

1. Decide which problems you think are most pressing (using the previous chapter).
2. Identify the best organizations within these areas, especially those that are especially limited by talent rather than funding. You can find a list of organizations within each of our problem profiles online, or in this list:

wiki.80000hours.org/index.php/Places_we_sometimes_r
ecommend_people_apply_to_work.
3. Find the positions where you'd have the best fit.

Which approach fits the problem?

We've now seen that by thinking broadly – considering earning to give, advocacy, and research as well as direct work – you can find many more ways to make a big contribution to pressing problems.

Hopefully that has given you some new ideas for jobs you could take. Now, how do you narrow these options down to find the best one?

The first thing to note is that these four approaches are not exclusive, and you can do more than one at the same time. For instance, a teacher helps their students (direct impact), but could also develop new educational techniques (research) or tell their students about pressing problems (advocacy). We know a teacher who did private tutoring in order to donate more (earning to give). As we've seen, often your impact is more about how you use your position than the position itself. This means, you'll want to look for the positions that offer the best balance of ways to contribute directly, through advocacy and through donations. In our career reviews, we assess each path on these three ways of contributing.

The second point is that there is no single best approach for every problem. Rather, focus on the approaches that are most needed by the problems you want to solve. For instance, breast cancer doesn't need more social advocacy to promote awareness, because almost everyone is aware that breast cancer is a problem. Instead, it probably needs more skilled researchers to develop better treatments. If you just focus on raising awareness, then your efforts won't go as far.

The Global Priorities Project has put together a flowchart which summarizes the best ways to make a difference. It's too large to reproduce here, but we recommend that you take a look at it here:

tinyurl.com/gmfbh46

But the most important thing is to find an option you're good at.

Do something where you have the chance to excel

Throughout this chapter, there is a vital general principle to bear in mind: *the most successful careers in a field have far more impact than the typical career.* This means the most effective approach *for you* will be one which is a good fit with your skills and motivation.

A landmark study of expert performers found:[34]

> *A small percentage of the workers in any given domain is responsible for the bulk of the work. Generally, the top 10% of the most prolific elite can be credited with around 50% of all contributions, whereas the bottom 50% of the least productive workers can claim only 15% of the total work, and*

---

[34] Simonton, Dean K. "Age and outstanding achievement: What do we know after a century of research?" Psychological bulletin 104.2 (1988): 251.

> *the most productive contributor is usually about 100*
> *times more prolific than the least.*

So if you were to plot degrees of success on a graph, it would look like this:

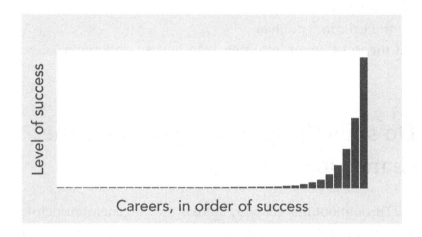

It's the same shape as the graphs we saw in the previous two chapters.

As we've seen, areas like research and advocacy are particularly extreme, but a major study still found that the best people in almost *any* field have significantly more output than the typical person.[35] The more complex the domain, the more significant the effect, so it's especially noticeable in professional jobs like management, sales, and medicine.

Now, some of these differences are just due to luck: even if everyone were an equally good fit, there could still be big differences in output just because some people happen to get

---

[35] Hunter, J. E., Schmidt, F. L., Judiesch, M. K., (1990) "Individual Differences in Output Variability as a Function of Job Complexity", Journal of Applied Psychology.

lucky while others don't. However, some component is due to skill, and this means you'll have much more impact if you choose an area where you have the potential to be good at it.

Moreover, success in almost any field gives you influence that can be turned into positive impact by using your position to advocate for important problems. So, an outstanding charity worker will likely do more good than a mediocre engineer earning to give, and the reverse is also true.

This all also means you should probably avoid taking a "high impact" option that you don't enjoy, and lacks the other ingredients of job satisfaction, like engaging work. If you don't enjoy the work, you're more likely to burn out and less likely to excel in the long-term.

So, once you have some ideas about high-impact paths to aim for long-term, our advice is to narrow them down based on job satisfaction and personal fit. We'll explain how in Chapter 6.

Conclusion: in which job can you help the most people?

There are many more paths to helping others in your career than we normally focus on. Bill Gates started as a software engineer, and saved millions of lives through earning to give. Rosa Parks was a seamstress, and helped to trigger the civil rights movement in America through advocacy. Alan Turing was a mathematician, and helped to end WW2 through research, as well as inventing the computer. Elon Musk is a businessman, but is helping to revolutionize the car and space industries to reduce risks to humanity's future.

Most people aren't Bill Gates, but even at a normal graduate salary, anyone can have an astonishing impact through earning to give, literally saving hundreds of lives. And it's often possible to do even more through advocacy, research or direct work.

Moreover, if you focus on the approaches that are best suited to the problems you want to solve, and where you have the best personal fit, you can do even more good again.

In this way, even if you don't want to be a doctor or a teacher, it's possible to do far more good with your career than is normally thought.

Recap of the guide so far

In Chapter 1, we saw that a fulfilling, dream job:

1. Helps others.
2. Is something you're good at.
3. Has the right supportive conditions (e.g. engaging work, fit with the rest of your life).

We also saw that to find a job which really helps others:

1. Work out **which problems are most pressing** – those that are big in scale, neglected and solvable – as we covered in Chapter 3.
2. Choose the **most effective approaches**. Think broadly by considering research, advocacy and earning to give as well as direct work, and choose the best approach for the problem.
3. Do something **you enjoy** where you have the **chance to excel**.

Should you sacrifice?

People often ask us whether they should sacrifice what they enjoy in order to have a greater impact. But we think doing good involves less sacrifice than it first seems. As we can see above, a personally satisfying job involves helping others, and a high impact job will also be personally satisfying. So there's a lot of overlap.

That's not to say there's no trade-off at all. It's highly unlikely that the best career for you personally is also the one that most benefits the world. Ultimately, you'll have to make a difficult to value judgement about how to weigh helping others against your own interests. However, the trade-off is much less than it first seems.

Apply this to your career

Before we move on, make an initial shortlist of fulfilling, high impact careers you could work towards in the long run. The following steps may help:

1. Decide which two to five problems you think are most pressing.
2. Find the relevant problem profiles on our website, read the list of career ideas in each profile, and note any that could be a good fit for you.
3. Go through the four approaches we covered in this chapter, and list out any other options that could be a good fit for you.

The aim at this point is just to come up with more options. We'll explain how to narrow down in later chapters.

If you're early in your career, try our career quiz

It's a six-question quiz that filters our recommended list of careers based on your answers:

http://80k.link/APT

If you already have experience, read our advice by area

wiki.80000hours.org/index.php/Advice_by_expertise

The bottom line: in which career can you do the most good?

- Once you've chosen a problem, as we covered in Chapter 3, the next step is to work out how best to contribute to solving it.
- Consider indirect approaches such as research, advocacy and earning to give, *as well as* direct work. You might be able to find a path that offers more influence, or that's a better fit for you.
- Then focus on the approaches that are most needed in your problem area. Some problems are best solved through changing policy. Others most need research, while others require funding, and so on.
- Finally, because the most successful people in a field achieve far more than the typical person, choose something where you have the potential to excel. Don't do something you won't enjoy in order to have more impact.
- Ultimately, look for the best option on a combination of (i) how pressing the problem is (ii) how large your contribution will be (iii) your degree of personal fit.

CHAPTER 5

Which jobs put you in the best position for the future? How to avoid two common early-career mistakes.

Kate wanted to make a difference, so she did the obvious thing – she went to work at a non-profit straight out of university. [36] However, she quickly hit a ceiling in terms of how far she could advance.

We've asked leaders of effective non-profits whether it makes sense to start your career in the non-profit sector. [37] They said you can usually advance faster in the corporate sector because you get better training. Moreover, they said that's where they hire from.

Kate ended up returning to the corporate sector for several years, and would have ended up ahead if she'd done that straight away. We know lots of examples of people who feel like they wasted years of their career.

---

[36] Not her real name.

[37] Full details of these discussions are at 80000hours.org/2015/09/what.

Don't make these mistakes. Although it's good to make a difference right away, you also need to invest in yourself to maximize your impact in the long-term, and find a job you're good at. This means building what we call "career capital": skills, connections and credentials that put you in a better position to make a difference in the future.

Furthermore, it's important to build career capital that's *flexible* – that will be relevant in many different jobs in the future.

By investing in their career capital, there's a huge amount anyone can do to put themselves in a better position to have a satisfying career and make a difference.

Mistake 1: Ignoring opportunities to invest in yourself

If you want to increase your social impact, you face a choice: try to make a difference right away, or invest in yourself to make a greater impact in the long-term. Which is best?

This is a complex question, and we have more research online,[38] but we think many people should focus on investing in themselves early in their career. Why?

People like to lionize the Mozarts and Mark Zuckerbergs of the world – people who achieved great success while young – and there are all sorts of awards for young leaders, like the Forbes 30 under 30. But these stories are interesting precisely because they're the exception.

---

[38] 80000hours.org/articles/should-you-wait

Most people reach the peak of their impact in their middle age. Income usually peaks in the 40s, suggesting that it takes around 20 years for most people to reach their peak productivity. Similarly, experts only reach their peak abilities between age 30 and 60, and if anything, this age is increasing over time.[39]

Field	Age of peak output
Theoretical physics, lyric poetry, pure mathematics	Around 30
Psychology, chemistry	Around 40
Novel writing, history, philosophy, medicine	Around 50
Business - average age of S&P500 CEOs	55
Politics - average age of first-term (US) presidents	55

[39] Guvenen, F., Karahan, F., Ozkan, S. and Song, J. "What Do Data on Millions of U.S. Workers Reveal about Life-Cycle Earnings Risk?" Staff Report No. 710 February 2015.

Simonton, Dean K. "Age and outstanding achievement: What do we know after a century of research?" Psychological Bulletin 104.2 (1988).

Snow, S. "These are the ages when we do our best work." Fast Company, 2016.

Jones, B., Reedy, E.J. and Weinberg, B. "Age and scientific genius." No. w19866. National Bureau of Economic Research, 2014.

When researchers looked in more detail at these findings, they found that expert-level performance in established fields requires 10-30 years of focused practice.[40]

K. Anders Ericsson, the leader of this field of research who has been working on it for over 30 years, said:

> *I have never found a convincing case for anyone developing extraordinary abilities without intense, extended practice.*

Mozart and Mark succeeded while young because they started young. Mozart's father was a famous music teacher, and trained him intensely as a toddler.

All this may sound like a bit of a downer, but consider the flip side. Lots of people come to us saying "I'm not sure I have any useful skills to contribute". And that's often true. If you've just graduated, you've probably spent the last four years studying Moby Dick, quantum mechanics, and Descartes, and your future job is unlikely to involve any of those things.

However, Ericsson's research suggests that *anyone* can improve at most skills with focused practice. Sure, talent is probably important too – if you're 7-foot-tall it's going to be a lot easier to learn basketball – but that doesn't mean short people can't still improve their game. This means even if you

---

[40] Ericsson, K. Anders, et al., eds. "The Cambridge handbook of expertise and expert performance." Cambridge University Press, 2006. Summarized in the author's new popular book, *"Peak"*.

Macnamara, Brooke N., David Z. Hambrick, and Frederick L. Oswald. "Deliberate practice and performance in music, games, sports, education, and professions: a meta-analysis." Psychological science 25.8 (2014): 1608-1618.

don't have much to contribute now, you can become much more skilled in the future.

In our advising, we've seen lots of examples of people becoming far more successful, happy and capable by investing in themselves. We'll cover some examples later.

All this means there's a good chance you can have a greater lifetime impact by first investing in yourself.

For this reason, our advice is to *always* be on the lookout for opportunities to build career capital.

However, career capital is especially important early in your career: the earlier you increase your abilities, the more time you have to make use of the increase, and the larger the total gain you'll get. So, early career, the ideal is to find a job that offers both impact and career capital, but if forced to choose between the two, lean towards career capital.

This doesn't mean ignoring social impact. It's best to stay involved through conferences, donating 1-10%, volunteering and so on, so you stay motivated and keep learning. Rather, the big issue at this point is where to put your focus.

However, career capital isn't only important in your twenties. As we saw, it takes 10-30 years to get to the top of a field, so you can keep improving your skills for decades. It depends on the quality of the opportunities you find to invest in yourself.

On the other hand, if you encounter an especially early urgent or opportunity, then it can make sense to prioritize impact over career capital, even if you're still early in your career. [41]

---

[41] 80000hours.org/articles/should-you-wait

How to compare two options in terms of career capital

Skills – what will you learn in this job? You can break skills down into transferable skills, knowledge and personality traits. Some especially useful transferable skills include: personal productivity, analysis and problem-solving, the ability to learn quickly, communication, data analysis, persuasion and negotiation, and management. If you want to do good, you also need to learn all about the world's most pressing problems. You'll learn fastest in jobs where you receive good mentorship.

Connections – who will you work with and meet in this job? Your connections are how you'll find opportunities, spread ideas and start new projects. The people you spend time with also shape your character (see section 5 of Appendix 2 for more detail). For both reasons, it's both important to make connections who are influential and who care about social impact.

Credentials – will this job act as a good signal to future collaborators or employers? Note that we don't just mean formal credentials like having a law degree, but also your achievements and reputation. If you're a writer, it's the quality of your blog. If you're a coder, it's your GitHub.

Runway – how much money will you save in this job? Your runway is how long you could comfortably live with no income. It depends on both your savings and how much you could reduce your expenses by. We recommend aiming for at least six months of runway to maintain your financial security. 12-18 months of runway is even more useful because it gives you the flexibility to make a major career change. It's usually worth paying down high-interest debt before donating more than 1% per year or taking a big pay cut for greater impact.

Mistake 2: Not building flexible career capital that will be useful in the future

What type of career capital should you gain?

Earlier we went looked at Kate, who went to work at a non-profit. Not only do non-profit jobs often build your skills more slowly, they're also less *flexible*. It's widely accepted in the non-profit sector that it's easier to switch from a business job to a non-profit job than vice versa. So if you're unsure between the two, a business position offers more flexibility.

Another cautionary tale is Topher, who was studying a philosophy PhD, but realized he probably wouldn't be able to get any academic positions that he was excited to pursue, and so left early and had to retrain. We've found lots of people start a humanities PhD and then realize they hate academia, and that their PhD won't help them much elsewhere. They end up feeling like they've near-wasted four years.

 **Example:** Tara trained and worked as a pharmacist with the Red Cross. Eventually she realized that she could have a greater impact elsewhere, but all the specialized knowledge she learned in pharmacy would no longer be useful. This is common when people choose specialized courses that are only really relevant to one path.

These examples show it's important not only to gain career capital, but to gain career capital that's *flexible* – useful in many different types of jobs – and likely to remain useful in the future. For instance, learning marketing or management is flexible because almost all organizations need these skills, whereas becoming an expert on Kenyan microfinance is not.

Flexibility is important firstly because it's really hard to know what the future holds. Many of the most in-demand jobs today, like being a data scientist or growth hacker, didn't even exist ten years ago. And it seems like the pace of change is going to be even faster in the coming decades.

Thinking of becoming a legal clerk, medical technician, or real estate broker? These jobs might soon be gone. Several decades ago, Chess was held up as an example of something a machine could never do. But in 1997, Kasparov was defeated by the computer program Deep Blue. Back in 2004, two experts in artificial intelligence used truck driving as an example of a job that would be really hard to automate.[42] Today, self-driving cars are already on the road. Back in 2014, Nick Bostrom predicted it would take ten years for a computer to beat the top human player at the ancient Chinese game of Go.[43] But it was achieved in March 2016 by Google Deep Mind.

In 2013, two researchers estimated that about half of all jobs are highly at risk of automation within the next twenty years. The most at-risk jobs include many "white collar" positions as well as manual jobs.[44]

---

[42] "The New Division of Labour" by Frank Levy and Richard Murnane (2004). Chapter 2 is titled "Why People Still Matter".

[43] "Superintelligence" by Nick Bostrom (2014).

[44] For more information see 80000hours.org/2015/02/which-careers-will-be-automated.

The safest jobs are those that involve creativity, high-level problem-solving, and social intelligence, such as: management, marketing, social work, and engineering.

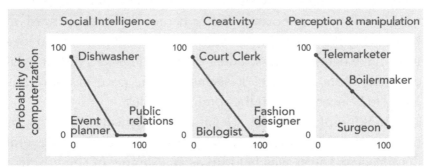

Taken from Frey, Carl Benedikt, and Michael A. Osborne, "The future of employment: how susceptible are jobs to computerization." Sept 17, 2013.

These technological changes, combined with global markets, are also increasing the rewards for being a top performer in your field. Think of WhatsApp, which has only 55 employees but over 700 million users (as of July 2016). It would never have been possible for such a small number of people to serve so many customers a few decades ago. These changes are not only limited to the technology sector; they're happening everywhere. JK Rowling became the highest-earning author of all time because Harry Potter became popular all around the world. These days, people work in a global market rather than a national one. This means the importance of building good career capital is actually increasing over time.

We've seen that it's important to build *flexible, future-proof* career capital because the world is changing so fast. But that's not all. *You're* also going to change. Research shows that people's interests change significantly, and more than they expect.[45] Think about your hobbies ten years ago. They're probably pretty different today.

You'll also keep learning more about which career paths are best.

Flexibility is *even more* important if you care about social impact, because it allows you to focus on whichever problems turn out to be most pressing in the future. In the 1960s, the big issue was nuclear war and hardly anyone had heard about climate change, whereas today climate change is widely seen as the bigger issue.

We're optimistic that global health will be much improved in twenty years, so it will be less pressing. On the other hand, we expect new problems to be discovered. This means it's probably better to give yourself the option to switch problem area in the future, even if it slightly reduces your impact in the short run.

In general, the more uncertain you are about the future, the more important it is to gain career capital that's flexible. One consequence of this is that flexibility is usually most important at the start of your career. At this point you haven't tried any jobs, so it's the point when you know the least about what you want to do in the future.

Bear in mind, the advice "build flexible career capital" is *not* the same as "don't close any doors". Some people try to avoid committing to a specific path because they're unsure what to do. Rather, the advice is to *commit* to a path in which you'll gain career capital that's useful in many other paths. Just pick an area, perform highly, learn transferable skills, and meet

---

[45] Quoidbach, J., Gilbert, D. T., & Wilson, T. D. (2013). The End of History Illusion. Science, 339(6115), 96-98.

influential people. You'll end up in a better position than if you try to do a bit of everything and don't achieve anything.

Which jobs are best early career?

So we've seen what career capital is and why it's important. But how do you get it? Here's a list of paths that we've found are often good for gaining flexible career capital early on. Note down any that could be a good fit for you. More information on each career path can be found in Appendix 8.

1. Work at a growing organization that has a reputation for high performance

Rob Mather is the founder of Against Malaria Foundation, which GiveWell rates as the most cost-effective, proven and well-run charity in the world (as of 2016). But he started his career in sales and management consulting. He says these positions gave him the management and persuasion skills he used to make AMF so lean and efficient.

Consulting isn't usually seen as the socially motivated choice. But if you're really unsure what to do long-term, it can work. Consultants go into a very wide range of areas, including the public and social sector, and often reach senior positions more quickly than they would if they hadn't started in consulting. The same can be true of other "professional services" jobs. If you're worried about getting "sucked in" to the lifestyle, then make a commitment to your friends to leave after a certain number of years.

Consulting works because the companies make you work hard, train you up, and put you around other productive people, building your skills and connections. These jobs are also widely recognized as competitive positions, which gives you a credential.

But there are many other positions that provide similar benefits. In fact, if you have a clearer idea about what you want to do long-term, then there's probably something better than consulting or professional services.

Moreover, *any* position where you have a good mentor or team can help you learn quickly. And any organization that is growing quickly can let you gain responsibility quickly.

Here are some of the most common types of options that seem promising. Try to identify the ones you'd be best at, and focus on those.

The following offer the most flexibility, so are best if you're especially uncertain:

- **The technology sector** – This sector attracts many of the most ambitious people, often leads other fields when it comes to best practices, is growing, and working in the sector can let you develop useful technical skills. See our profiles on software engineering, data science, startup early employee and startup founder.

- **Management consulting** – If you're really uncertain, management consulting, especially strategy consulting, can be a good option. These firms often invest heavily in training, and you meet lots of other high-performers, while exploring lots of industries. Management consultants exit into almost all sectors.

- **Professional services** – This includes accounting and other advisory services, and most often involves working at the Big 4: Deloitte, Ernst and Young, PwC and KPMG. This path provides similar benefits to management consulting, but is less competitive, as well as less prestigious and with a weaker range of exit options.

- **Work in a small but rapidly growing company with a good boss.** You'll get to try out lots of areas, learn quickly and advance rapidly.

The following are especially relevant to a certain area, but also good general first steps:

- **Government position leadership schemes**, such as the Fast Stream in the UK, or Presidential Management Fellowship in the US. These are especially good options if you want to work anywhere in the policy world or social sector.

- **Think tank research roles** are reasonably prestigious, and open up options in policy and the social sector.

- **Working for a politician** (e.g. as a researcher or staffer) is often the first step into political and policy positions. It's also demanding, prestigious and gives you lots of connections.

- **Positions in major media companies**, because you build communications skills and connections, and these jobs are often prestigious.

- **Teaching accelerator schemes**, such as Teach for America and Teach First, because they're highly demanding and focus on rapid training. Though, if you know you don't want to enter the education sector, other options are probably better.

- **Top non-profits**, such as Evidence Action and GiveWell. Although the typical non-profit isn't usually the best option for career capital, if you can join an effective team, or take a role where you'll learn a lot, it can still be a top option. Working at a non-profit is also better for developing a network of people who care about social impact.

- Anywhere you can work with a **high-achieving mentor**.

Law and investment banking are also common options for career capital, and have similar characteristics to consulting. If you have relatively better verbal skills, law is likely to be the better fit. If you have relatively better social skills, then consider the "dealmaking" positions in investment banking, such as mergers and acquisitions. If you have relatively better quantitative skills, then consider sales and trading or asset management in investment banking.

In general, however, we prefer consulting to these options because: (i) it's growing, whereas these industries are flat and have a worse outlook (ii) it seems to give you a wider range of options (iii) the work is often more engaging at the early levels (though often still boring!) (iv) you get to explore several industries (v) there's better arguments that some parts of law and banking are harmful. Law also requires an expensive up-front investment.

However, consulting is lower paid, so if you're relatively set on earning to give and a good fit for either of law or investment banking, it might make sense to enter them (and focus on a non-harmful area).

Example: David wasn't sure what to do with his life. He seriously considered pursuing a PhD in international relations, but decided academia wasn't for him. He worked in finance, started and sold a business, then worked for Founder's Forum for Good, a network of entrepreneurs who want to further social change. Eventually he hit on the idea of getting startup entrepreneurs to pledge some of their shares to charity. The network of entrepreneurs and credibility he had developed gave him access to the right people. The sales skills he had learned enabled him to convince his connections. In under a year, he raised $70 million of legally binding pledges, and is advising the entrepreneurs on the most effective places to donate.

2. Pursue certain graduate studies

If you want to work in academic research, a think tank or law, then you'll probably have to go to graduate school. But if you're not confident about pursuing one of these areas, can it be worth pursuing graduate study for general career capital?

Our preliminary answer is yes, but only if it's a program that gives you good backup options in case academia doesn't work out. For instance, the most attractive grad program might be an economics PhD:

1. Almost all economics PhDs can get jobs involving economics if they want, which is not the case with most doctorates.
2. Economics is an especially important area of academia for people who care about social impact.

3. You can go from economics into the rest of the social sciences; plus economists can go into important positions in policy, and they have high-earning corporate backup options.

On the other hand, people often drift into expensive graduate programs that don't offer good back-up options (e.g. philosophy PhD), even if they're not sure about academia. This is not usually a good move.

How can you compare your options for graduate studies? Weigh up your options in terms of:

1. **Personal fit** – will you be good at the subject? If you're good at the area, it's more likely you'll be able to pursue work in that area later on, you'll enjoy it more, and you'll do the work more quickly.

2. **Flexibility of the program** – does it open up lots of options, both inside and outside academia? If you're uncertain about academia, watch out for programs that mainly help you with academic careers (e.g. philosophy PhD, literature PhD). If you do a math PhD you can transfer into economics, physics, biology, computer science and so on, but the reverse is not true. Also some graduate programs give you better odds of landing academic positions (e.g. 90%+ of economists can get research positions, whereas only about 50% of biology PhDs do).

3. **Relevance to your long-term plans** – does it take you towards the options you're most interested in? Lots of people are tempted to do graduate study even when it doesn't particularly help with their longer-term plans. For instance, potential entrepreneurs are tempted to do

MBAs when they're not particularly helpful to entrepreneurship; lots of people are tempted to do a random Master's degree when they're not sure what to do; some people consider doing a law degree when they're not confident they want to be a lawyer.

Besides economics, some graduate subjects we especially recommend considering:

- Computer science
- Applied math (and anything that involves a lot of applied math)
- We suspect there are more – like certain business degrees – but we haven't investigated them yet.

But don't take a graduate program that you'll hate. Rather, look for an option that has a good combination of personal fit, flexibility and relevance to your long-term plans.

Example: Dillon couldn't imagine studying anything except philosophy. Then he found out about the research that shows that our interests can easily change. Convinced, he decided to try out economics and computer science as minor courses, because he thought these would open up more options than philosophy. He liked them more than he expected, and now intends to do a PhD in Economics.

3. Develop a valuable, transferable skill

Any option that gives you a provable, useful, transferable skill can be a good move. Some concrete options that fall into this category include:

Programming bootcamp – We know lots of examples of people who started with no technology background, and within six months ended up with highly paid programming jobs they enjoy far more than their old jobs. Programming is also a growing, in-demand skill that can be used in many areas. Bootcamps are intensive, three-month programs that aim to get you a job as soon as possible. They often have over 90% placement rates, and some are free unless you get a job. For more about this skill, see our review of software engineering.

Data science bootcamp – Data science is a cross between statistics and programming. The bootcamps are a similar deal to programming, although they tend to mainly recruit science PhDs. If you've just done a science PhD and don't want to continue with academia, this is a good option to consider. For more, see our full review of data science. Similarly you can learn data analysis, statistics and modeling by taking the right graduate program, as discussed above.

Marketing and sales – Learning to market toilet paper doesn't seem like the most socially motivated option. But almost all types of organization need marketing, and demand for the skill is growing. You can learn the skill-set, then transfer into an organization with a social mission. Failing that, the skill has high market value, so you could earn to give instead.

Marketing skills can be learned by taking an entry-level position at a top firm or working under a good mentor in a business. We'd especially recommend focusing on the more technology-driven marketing that's sometimes called "growth hacking". Read more in our career review of marketing.

Example: Having studied political science, and decided against graduate study, Peter wasn't sure what to do. He considered law and working at a charity. But instead he taught himself to program and became a data scientist at a startup, because this allowed him to gain better career capital.

4. Do what contributes

A common mistake at this point is to think that building career capital always means doing something that gives you formal credentials, like a law degree, or doing something prestigious, like consulting.

It's easy to focus on "hard" aspects of career capital, like having a brand-name employer, because they're concrete; but the "soft" aspects of career capital – your skills, achievements, connections and reputation – are equally important, if not more so. The very best career capital comes from impressive achievements.

This is why starting your own organization can sometimes be the best path for career capital. If you succeed, it'll be impressive. Even if you don't succeed, you'll learn a lot, and might meet lots of interesting people. So if you're really motivated by a new project you think is important, then seriously consider it as a route to career capital.

But you don't need to become an entrepreneur. You can build these "soft" aspects of career capital in almost any job if you perform well. Doing great work builds your reputation, and that allows you to make connections with other high achievers. If you push yourself to do great work, then you'll probably learn more too.

There are plenty of cases where someone has turned success in one field into success in another by using the reputation and connections they gained. For instance, Sheryl Sandberg started in consulting, then worked in the Treasury, and is now COO at Facebook. Arnold Schwarzenegger turned success in bodybuilding into success as a movie star, which he turned into success as a politician.

This means it's worth considering any area where you have good fit, even if it doesn't seem like a good option for career capital in general. We'll cover how to assess personal fit in the next chapter.

If you care about social impact, then it's especially good to have achievements that involve doing good. Most importantly, it'll mean you meet people who deeply care about social impact, and that will be more useful than knowing lots of accountants.

The best example of this we know might be Niel Bowerman, who we met earlier. He really cared about climate advocacy while at university. This motivated him to improve his advocacy skills and brought him in contact with great people, and that led to impressive achievements, such as founding a think tank. Today, however, he works on other risks to the future, like pandemics rather than climate change. He was able to transfer his success into another area.

As we've seen, doing what contributes is a good strategy both for helping others and being personally satisfied. Now, it turns out it can also be a good strategy for building career capital. If you try to do what's most important for the world, you'll learn skills that are useful for helping others, gain impressive achievements, and make the right connections.

How can you get flexible career capital in any job?

Just as you can have an impact in *any* job by donating or using your influence, you can build career capital in any job.

There's a huge amount written about how to learn new skills and become more productive. You can find a list of resources in Appendix 2. For now, here are a couple of points to highlight.

We find many high achievers don't take care of themselves. The basics – sleep, diet, exercise, mental health and supportive friendships – make a huge difference to your happiness and productivity. So if there's anything easy you can do to improve these areas, it's usually worth it.

Around 20% of people each year experience a mental health problem. We know people who took the time to focus intensely on dealing with serious mental health problems and who, having found treatments and techniques that worked, have gone on to perform at the highest level. It's one of the best investments you can make in yourself.

The basics, however, are just a starting point. Any job can be an opportunity to build connections and learn useful skills.

Regular career advice focuses on the standard lists of transferable skills, like communication and data analysis, but the first area to focus on is skills that are useful in *all* jobs. There are lots of habits that can make you more productive no matter what you're doing. One simple example is the habit of writing down your top priority for the next day every evening, then doing it first thing. Check out the book *Deep Work* by Cal Newport for more ideas, as well as the resources in section 6 of Appendix 2.

Modern research also shows that it's possible to learn new skills much faster than you did at school. Learning how to learn is another example of a highly flexible skill that doesn't get discussed in regular careers advice. It'll help you succeed however the world changes, and it's becoming more important as technological change accelerates. In fact, learning how to learn is the ultimate skill because it'll help you learn everything else. To get started, see Barbara Oakley's work, including her Coursera course, *Learning How to Learn.*

A third example is rational thinking. Recent research shows that intelligence and rationality are distinct,[46] but rationality is much easier to train. Being able to think well and make good decisions is vital in all jobs. But it's even more important if you want to engage with the complex challenges of making the world a better place. The Center for Applied Rationality is using the research on rationality to develop practical training programs, especially for people who want to have an impact, and they usually offer discounts to readers of 80,000 Hours.

For more tips, including advice on how to network, see Appendix 2.

Conclusion

You may not be sure how best to contribute today, and you may suspect that you have few valuable skills, but that's fine.

Although we like stories of those who achieved apparently instant fame and early success, like the Forbes 30 under 30, it's

---

[46] For a summary of some of this research, see:
http://www.nytimes.com/2016/09/18/opinion/sunday/the-difference-between-rationality-and-intelligence.html

not the norm. Behind most great achievements are many years spent diligently building expertise.

We've seen people transform their careers by doing things like learning to program, finding the right boss, moving to a city where they can build good connections, and getting the right PhD.

If you focus on building valuable, flexible career capital, then you'll be able to have a more impactful, satisfying career too.

Apply this to your own career

1. **Go over all the four paths to career capital and ways to gain career capital in any job**, and note down three new ways you could gain career capital.

   a. Can you work at a high-performance, growing organization?

   b. Do you have a good option for graduate study?

   c. Can you do something that will teach you a valuable skill?

   d. Is there an option where you'll achieve something impressive, especially if relevant to social impact?

2. **Read the list of ways to gain career capital in any job** in Appendix 2. Choose one to focus on over the next year.

3. **What's the most valuable career capital you already have?** Identifying your most valuable career capital can give you clues about what you'll be best at, and help you to convince employers to hire you. Review each of the categories:

   a. Skills, which you can break down into (i) transferable skills, (ii) knowledge, and (iii) personality traits.

   b. Connections

   c. Credentials,

   d. Runway.

If you're stuck, list out the five achievements you're most proud of, and ask what they have in common.

4. **If you're early in your career, take our career quiz** (http://80k.link/APT). Select "early career" and it'll mainly rank options by their potential for career capital.

5. **If you're later in your career, take a look at our advice by area**:
wiki.80000hours.org/index.php/Advice_by_expertise

6. **To read more**, check out *So Good They Can't Ignore You* by Cal Newport (where we learned the term "career capital").

The bottom line: which jobs put you in the best position for the future?

Career capital is anything that puts you in a better position to make a difference in the future, including skills, connections, credentials, and runway.

Gaining career capital is important throughout your career, but especially when you're young and you have a lot to learn.

The earlier you are in your career, and the less certain you are about what to do in the medium term, the more you should focus on gaining career capital that's *flexible*, i.e. useful in many different sectors and career paths.

Some of the best ways to get career capital early on include:

- Working in any organization which has, or with any people who have, a reputation for high performance, e.g. top consultancy or technology firms, or any work with a great mentor or team.
- Undertaking certain graduate studies, especially applied quantitative subjects like economics, computer science and applied mathematics.
- Anything that gives you a valuable transferable skill, e.g. programming, data science, marketing.
- Taking opportunities which allow you to achieve impressive, socially valuable things, e.g. founding an organization, doing anything at which you

might excel.

You can also build career capital in any situation by taking care of yourself, building connections and learning useful skills, especially skills that are relevant in every job, like learning how to learn.

CHAPTER 6

How to find the right career for you

Everyone knows it's important to find a job you're good at, but how do you do that?

The standard advice is to think about it for weeks and weeks until you "realize your talent". To help, career advisers give you quizzes about your interests and preferences. Others recommend you go on a gap year, reflect deeply, imagine different options, and try to figure out what truly motivates you.

But as we saw in the previous chapter, becoming really good at most skills takes decades of practice. So, to a large degree your abilities are built rather than "discovered". Darwin, Lincoln, JK Rowling and Oprah all failed early in their career, then went on to completely dominate their fields. Albert Einstein's 1895 schoolmaster's report reads, "He will never amount to anything."

Asking "what am I good at?" needlessly narrows your options. It's better to ask: "what could I *become* good at?"

That aside, the bigger problem is that these methods don't work. Plenty of research shows that it's really hard to predict what you'll be good at ahead of time, especially just by "going with your gut", and it turns out career tests don't work either.

Instead, the best way to find the right career for you is to *go investigate* – learn about and try out your options, looking outwards rather than inwards. Here we'll explain how.

Being good at your job is more important than you think

Everyone agrees that it's important to find a job you're good at. But we think it's *even more* important than most people think.

As we've seen, the most successful people in a field account for a large fraction of the impact, so you'll have much more impact if you find a job you can really excel at (Chapter 4). You're also likely to be happier (Chapter 1), and you'll build up more impressive achievements, and so gain better career capital (Chapter 5).

That's why *personal fit* is one of the key factors to look for in a job. We think of "personal fit" as your chances of excelling at a job, if you work at it.

Personal fit is like a multiplier of everything else. So, if we put together everything we've covered so far, this would be our formula for a perfect job:

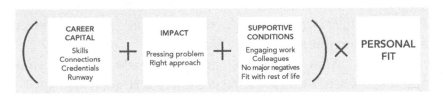

If you're comparing two career options, you can use these factors to make a side-by-side comparison.

Personal fit is important. In fact, it's probably more important than the other three factors, so we'd never recommend taking a "high impact" job that you'd be bad at. But how can you figure out where you'll have the best personal fit?

Hopefully you have some ideas for long-term options (from Chapter 4). Now we'll explain how to narrow them down, and find the right career for you.

Why self-reflection won't work

Performance is unpredictable

Advice like "go with your gut" or "follow your heart" assumes you can work out what you're going to be good at ahead of time. But in fact, you can't.

Here's the best study we've been able to find on how to predict performance in different jobs. It's a meta-analysis of selection tests used by employers, drawing on hundreds of studies performed over 85 years.[47] Here are some of the results:

Type of selection test	Correlation with job performance (r)
Work sample tests	0.54
IQ tests	0.51

---

[47] Schmidt, Frank L., and John E. Hunter. "The validity and utility of selection methods in personnel psychology: Practical and theoretical implications of 85 years of research findings." Psychological bulletin 124.2 (1998): 262.

Interviews (structured)	0.51
Peer ratings	0.49
Job knowledge tests	0.48
Job tryout procedure	0.44
Integrity tests	0.41
Interviews (unstructured)	0.38
Job experience	0.18
Years of education	0.1
Holland-type match	0.1
Graphology	0.02
Age	-0.01

Note that *none of the tests are very good*. A correlation of 0.5 is pretty weak, so even if you try to predict using the best available techniques, you're going to be "wrong" much of the time: candidates that look bad will often turn out good, and vice versa. Anyone who's hired people before will tell you that's exactly what happens.

Because hiring is so expensive, employers *really* want to pick the best candidates and they know exactly what the job requires. If even they, using the best available tests, can't figure out who's going to perform best in advance, you probably don't have much chance.

Don't go with your gut

If you were to try to predict performance in advance, "going with your gut" doesn't seem like the best way to do it. Research in the science of decision-making collected over several decades shows that intuitive decision-making only works in certain circumstances.[48]

For instance, your gut instinct can tell you very rapidly if someone is angry with you. This is because our brain is biologically wired to rapidly warn us when in danger.

Your gut can also be amazingly accurate when trained. Chess masters have an astonishingly good intuition for the best moves, and this is because they've trained their intuition by playing lots of similar games, and built up a sense of what works and what doesn't.

However, gut decision-making is poor when it comes to working out things like how fast a business will grow, who will win a football match, and what grades a student will receive. In Chapter 1, we also saw our intuition is poor at working out what will make us happy.

Career decision-making is more like these examples than being a chess grandmaster. It's hard to train our gut instinct when: (i) the results of our decisions take a long time to arrive, (ii) we have few opportunities to practice, or (iii) the situation keeps changing. This is exactly the situation with career choices: we only make a couple of major career decisions in our

---

[48] See our full evidence review at 80000hours.org/articles/dont-go-with-your-gut-instinct. We also recommend Daniel Kahneman's excellent book "Thinking Fast and Slow".

life, it takes years to see the results, and the job market keeps changing.

This all means your gut can give you *clues* about the best career. It can tell you things like "I don't trust this person" or "I'm not excited by this project". But you can't simply "go with your gut".

Why career tests also don't work

Many career tests are built on "Holland-types" or something similar. These tests classify you as one of six Holland-types, like "artistic" or "enterprising". Then they recommend careers that match that type. However, we can see from the table that "Holland-type match" is very weakly correlated with performance. It's also barely correlated with job satisfaction. So that's why we don't recommend traditional career tests.

What *does* work in predicting performance?

In the table, the tests that best predict performance are those that are closest to *actually doing the work* (with the interesting exception of IQ). This is probably what we should have expected.

A work sample test is simply doing some of the work, and having the results evaluated by someone experienced. Peer ratings measure what your peers think of your performance (and so can only be used for internal promotions). Job tryout procedures and job knowledge tests are pretty self-explanatory.

So the key to figuring out what you're good at is actually trying things. That's the first reason why our motto for working out personal fit is: *go investigate*.

To find the right career for you, go investigate

To really work out what you'll be good at, you need to speak to people, learn about the options and try things out. The closer you can get to actually doing the work, the better.

So, when deciding between your options, first take some time to really research them. This is true whether you're planning what to do long-term, comparing two offers, or considering quitting your job. With some decisions the stakes aren't high enough to warrant much research. But career decisions will influence years of your life, so are worth weeks of work.

Second, eventually you'll need to go out and try things. Especially if you're early in your career, or just very uncertain, consider trying out your top two to four long-term options over the next two to five years. For instance, if long-term you're considering being an engineer or being a writer, maybe you could study engineering and spend one afternoon per week writing a blog.

Also consider trying one or two *wildcards* to broaden your experience and spot new ideas. These are unusual options out of the normal path, like living in a new country, pursuing an unusual side project or trying a sector you would have not normally worked in (e.g. government, non-profits, social enterprise).

Why "go investigate"?

First, as we've seen, it's the best way to learn what you're good at.

Moreover, as a strategy, it makes sense to spend the first part of your career learning more. Early on you know relatively little about your strengths and options. Once you've spent a few years learning more, you'll be able to make better decisions over the coming decades.

Many successful people did exactly that. Tony Blair worked as a rock promoter before going into politics. As we saw, Condoleezza Rice was a classical musician before she entered politics; while Steve Jobs even spent a year in India on acid, and considered moving to Japan to become a Zen monk.

Today, it's widely accepted that many people will work in several sectors and roles across their lifetime. The typical 25 to 34-year-old changes jobs every three years, and changes are not uncommon later too.

The final reason is to avoid one of the biggest career mistakes: considering too few options. We've met lots of people who stumbled into paths like PhDs, medicine or law because they felt like the default at the time, but who, if they had considered more options, could easily have found something that fit them better. Pushing yourself to try out several areas will help you to avoid this mistake. Try to settle on a single goal too early, however, and you could miss a great option.

All this said, exploring can still be costly. Trying out a job can take several years, and changing job too often makes you look flaky. How can you explore, while keeping the costs low?

How to narrow down your options

You can't try everything, so before you explore, we need to cut your ideas for long-term options down to a shortlist.

How best to narrow down? Since gut decision-making is unreliable, it helps to be a little systematic.

Many people turn to pro and con lists, but these have some weaknesses. First, there's no guarantee the pros and cons that come to mind will be the most important aspects of the decision. Second, pro and con lists don't force you to look for disconfirming evidence or generate more options, and these are some of the most powerful ways to make better decisions. It's easy to use lists of pros and cons to rationalize what you already believe.

Here's the process for narrowing down that we recommend. It's based on a literature review of decision-making science and what has worked well in one-on-one advising. You can also use it when you need to compare options to shortlist, or compare your current job against alternatives.

1. **Make a big list of options.**
   a. Write out your initial list, including both what problem you want to focus on and what role you want e.g. economics researcher focusing on global health; marketing for a meat substitutes company, earning to give as a software engineer.
   b. Then force yourself to come up with more. You can find ideas in Chapter 3 and 4. But here are some questions to help you think of more: (i) If you couldn't take any of the options on your first list, what would you do? (ii) If money were no object, what would you do? (iii) What do your friends advise? (iv) (If already with experience) how could you use your most valuable career capital? (v) Can you combine your options to make the best of both worlds? (vi) Can you find any more opportunities through your connections?

2. **Rank your options.**
   a. Start by making an initial guess.
   b. If you have more time, then score your options from one to five, based on (i) impact, (ii) personal fit, (iii) other elements of job satisfaction, (iv) any other factors that are important to you. If you're considering options for the short-term, then also rate on career capital. Doing this ensures you're focusing on the most important factors. You can find tips on how to assess each factor in the "decision framework" article in Appendix 4.
   c. Then try to cut down to a shortlist. Eliminate the options that are worse on all factors than another ("dominated options"), and those that are very poor on one factor. You can add up all your scores to get a very rough ranking of options. If one of your results seems odd, try to understand why. For each option, ask "why might I be wrong?" and adjust your ranking. This is a very useful way to reduce bias.

3. **Key uncertainties.** What information could most easily change your ranking? If you could get the answer to one question, which question would be most useful? Write these out. E.g. "Can I get a place on Teach for America?", "Would I enjoy programming?", "How pressing is global poverty compared to open science?". If you're stuck, imagine you had to decide your career in just one weekend – what would you do in that time to make the right choice?

4. **Initial research.** Can you quickly work out any of these key uncertainties? E.g. if you're unsure whether you'd enjoy being a data scientist, can you go and talk to

someone about what it's like? Or is there something you could read, like one of our career reviews?

At this point, you might have a clear winner, in which case you can skip the next part. Most people, however, end up with a couple of alternatives that look pretty good. At that point, it's time to explore. But how best to do that?

How to explore: cheap tests first

We often find people who want to try out economics, so they go and apply for a Master's course. But that's a huge investment. Instead, think about how you can learn more with the least possible effort: "cheap tests".

You can think of making a "ladder" of tests. For instance, if you're interested in policy advising, here are the steps you might take:

- Read our relevant career reviews and do some Google searches to learn the basics (1-2h).

- Then the next most useful thing you can usually do is to speak to someone in the area. The right person can give you far more up-to-date and personalized information than what you'll be able to find written down (2h).

- Speak to three more people who work in the area and read one or two books (20h). You could also consider speaking to a careers advisor who specializes in this area. During this, also find out the most effective way for you to enter the area, given your background. Bear in mind that when you're talking to these people, they are also informally interviewing you – see our advice on preparing for interviews in Chapter 8.

- Now look for a project that might take 1-4 weeks of work, like volunteering on a political campaign, or starting a blog on the policy area you want to focus on. If you've done the previous step, you'll know what's best.

- Only now consider taking on a 2-24 month commitment, like a short work placement, internship or graduate study. At this point, being offered a trial position with an organization for a couple of months can actually be an advantage, because it means both parties will make an effort to quickly assess your fit.

At each point, you'd re-evaluate whether policy advising was one of your most promising options, and only continue to the next step if it is.

How to explore: order your options well

When trying out lots of options over several years, it's important to put them in the right order.

1. Explore before graduate study rather than after

In the two years after you graduate, you have license to try out something unusual.

It's an especially good opportunity because if it doesn't go well, you can use the "graduate school reset": do a Masters, MBA or PhD, then return to the traditional path.

Moreover, at the end of a PhD it's very hard to leave academia. This is because going from a PhD to a post-doc, and then into a permanent academic position is very competitive, and it's very unlikely you'll succeed if you don't focus 100% on research. So, if you're unsure about academia, try out alternatives before your PhD if possible.

2. Put "reversible" options first

For instance, it's easier to go from a position in business to a non-profit job than vice versa, so if you're unsure between the two, take the business position first.

3. Choose options that let you experiment

An alternative approach is to take a job that lets you try out several areas by:

- Letting you work in a variety of industries — freelance and consulting positions are especially good.
- Letting you practice many different skills – jobs in small companies are often especially good on this front.
- Giving you the free time and energy to explore other things outside of work.

4. Try on the side

If you're already in a job, think of ways to try out the new option on the side. Could you do a short project in your spare time, or in your existing job that's relevant? At the very least, speak to lots of people in the job.

If you're a student, try to do as many internships and summer projects as possible. Your university holidays are one of the best opportunities in your life to explore.

5. Keep building flexible career capital

If you're unsure, keep building flexible career capital. That way, no matter how things turn out, you'll still be in a better position in the future.

Jess – a case study in exploring

When Jess graduated from math and philosophy a couple of years ago, she was interested in academia and leaned towards studying philosophy of mind, but was concerned that it would have little impact.

So the year after she graduated, she spent several months working in finance. She didn't think she'd enjoy it, and she turned out to be right, so she felt confident eliminating that option. She also spent several months working in non-profits, and reading about different research areas.

Most importantly, she spoke to lots of people, especially in the areas of academia she was most interested in. This eventually led to her being offered to study a PhD in psychology, focused on how to improve decision-making by policy makers.

During her PhD, she did an internship at a leading evidence-based policy think tank, and started writing about psychology for an online newspaper. This meant that she was exploring the 'public intellectual' side of being an academic, and the option of going into policy.

At the end of her PhD, she can either continue in academia, or switch into policy or writing. She could also probably go back to finance or the non-profit sector. Most importantly, she'll have a far better idea of which options are best.

Conclusion

We like to imagine we can work out what we're good at through reflection, in a flash of insight. But that's not how it works.

Rather, it's more like a scientist testing a hypothesis. You have ideas about what you can become good at (hypotheses), which you can test out (experiments). Think you could be good at writing? Then start blogging. Think you'd hate consulting? At least speak to a consultant.

If you don't already know your "calling" or your "passion", that's normal. It's too hard to predict which career is right for you when you're starting out.

Instead, go and try things. You'll learn as you go, heading step-by-step towards a more fulfilling career.

Now let's tie together everything we've covered so far, and make sure you avoid the most common career planning mistakes.

Apply this to your own career: how to work out which career is right for you

1. Use the process above to narrow down your options to a shortlist of three to five.

2. For each option in your shortlist, write out one or two cheap tests. Do these in the next month or two.

3. Then, if you wanted to try out your remaining top options, what would the best order be? Consider just planning to spend several years trying out different areas.

4. When you need to make your final decision, you can use the narrowing down process again. The difference is that at the end you'll have to make your best guess at the top option, rather than exploring more.

5. If you'd like to find out more about how to make good decisions and predictions, we recommend *Decisive* by Chip and Dan Heath, and *Superforecasting* by Philip Tetlock.

The bottom line: how to find the right career for you

- Research shows that it's really hard to work out what you're going to be good at ahead of time, especially through self-reflection or going with your gut.

- Instead, *go investigate*. After an initial cut-down of your options, go learn more and then try them out.

- Minimize the costs of trying out your options by doing cheap tests first (usually start by speaking to people), then trying your options in the best order (e.g. business jobs before non-profit jobs).

- Keep adapting your plan over time. Think like a scientist investigating a hypothesis.

CHAPTER 7

How to make your career plan

People often come to us trying to figure out what they should do over the next ten or twenty years. Others come to us saying they want to figure out "the right career for them".

The problem with all of this is that your plan is almost certainly going to change:

1. You'll change (more than you think).
2. The world will change – as we saw, many industries around today won't even exist in twenty years.
3. You'll learn more about what's best for you. As we saw in the previous chapter, it's very hard to predict what you're going to be good at ahead of time.

In a sense, there is no single "right career for you". Rather, the best option will keep changing as the world changes and you learn more. As a result, trying to make a ten-year plan is unhelpful because the situation will change. It could even make you inflexible to new information and options.

On the other hand, you don't want to bungle around without any plan at all. Having specific goals will make you more likely to succeed, and thinking about which career options are best is better than sending out CVs at random.[49]

So what's the answer? A flexible plan.

Here we'll explain how to take your shortlist of options from the previous chapter and make a plan that's both specific and flexible.

The A/B/Z plan

Here's a template for writing career plans that we've found useful. You can use it to plan out the next couple of years wherever you are in your career.

The format is borrowed from business strategy from *The Start-Up of You*, a career advice book by the founder of LinkedIn, Reid Hoffman. Business strategy is similar to career strategy, because the situation is uncertain and rapidly changing. We've also tested several types of career plan with thousands of users, and this is our current favorite.

The idea of the A/B/Z plan is to set out a number of possible options, ranked according to preference. We've also added some adjustments depending on how confident you are about what's best.

1. Plan A – top option

This is the ideal scenario. You have three main options for your Plan A. Choose one of the following depending on how confident you are in what to aim for long-term.

---

[49] See our review of the value of setting goals 80000hours.org/2013/03/should-you-plan-your-career.

Option #1. If you're reasonably confident about your best long-term option, work out how you intend to get there.

Try to determine the best route to your top option by talking to people in the field and looking at what successful people have done in the past. In particular, look for exceptions - how have people got to these positions unusually fast, or despite major setbacks? Also double check the advice in our career reviews.

In addition, look for steps that both take you towards the goal and build flexible career capital at the same time. That way, even if your Plan A doesn't work out, you'll still have options. Use the advice in Chapter 5 on which options build flexible career capital.

Option #2. If you're uncertain about your best medium-term option, instead make a plan to try out your top 2-4 options over the next couple of years.

You can minimize the costs of trying out options by using the tips in the previous chapter, such as putting your options in the right order.

Option #3. If you're very uncertain about your best long-term option, then you need to (i) do more research (ii) in the meantime, build flexible career capital.

Give yourself a set amount of time for research. If you haven't done much research before, choose a short time frame like two months. If you've already done a lot of thinking, then you may just need to commit to one option for 1-3 years, then re-evaluate after that.

For the time you've set aside for research, create a list of ways to learn more which option is best.

Otherwise, do whatever will best build flexible career capital. Use the advice in Chapter 5.

If you're early in your career, you'll probably be in one of the last two categories. That's fine, you don't need to have it all figured out already.

If you need help coming up with longer-term options, then go back to Chapter 4, or use the brainstorming questions in Chapter 6. If you need help doing an initial narrow-down of those options, go back to Chapter 6.

2. Plan B – nearby alternatives

These are the options you could switch into if Plan A doesn't work out, and options that might easily turn out to be better than your Plan A. Writing them out ahead of time helps you to stay ready for new opportunities.

To sort out your Plan B, ask yourself what's most likely not to work with Plan A, and what obstacles you're most likely to face. Then figure out what you could do if this happens. Come up with two or three alternatives.

3. Plan Z – your temporary fallback

This is what you'll do if everything goes wrong to buy yourself time to get back on your feet. It might mean sleeping on a friend's sofa while paying the bills through tutoring or working at a café; living off savings; or going back to your old job. It could even mean something more adventurous like going to teach English in Asia – a surprisingly in-demand, uncompetitive job that lets you learn about a new culture.

Having a Plan Z makes it easier to take risks. If you think about it, Plan Z probably isn't so bad. You'll still have food, friends, a soft bed, and a room at the perfect temperature – better conditions than most people have faced in all history.

If you do face serious risks, however, such as having people who depend on your income, then you'll want to seriously consider what you would do if Plan A and B don't work out.

Knowing the downside makes it less scary, and having a back-up plan makes it more likely you'll cope.

An example career plan

Suppose that in the medium-term you're interested in doing development economics research or founding an international development non-profit, but you're unsure how good a fit you'll be for academia.

Then your plan could be:

- **Plan A:** While a student, spend a summer holiday living in a developing country (something you need to do to go into development) and another working at a non-profit. Then work as a consultant for two years, and then pursue a Master's in Economics. At that point, you'll either be able to continue in economics academia, or switch into non-profits.
- **Plan B:** You might not get a consulting job. In that case, you can go to grad school a year earlier, and spend your year out interning at a non-profit, or teaching English in a developing country.
- **Plan Z:** Move back in with your parents and take a job at the deli you worked at last summer.

Commit to reviewing your plan

Your plan should change as you learn more, but it's easy to get stuck on the path you're already on. Not changing course when a better option exists is one of the most common decision-making mistakes identified by psychologists, and is called the "sunk cost fallacy" or "status quo bias".

To help avoid this mistake, you need to keep reviewing your plan. Here are a few ideas:

- Schedule in a time to review your career in six months or a year. We have a short career review tool on our website to make that easy.[50] Work through the questions by yourself, and then try to justify your thoughts to a friend or mentor. Other people are better able to spot the sunk cost bias, and having to justify your thinking to someone else has been shown to reduce your degree of bias.[51]
- Set check-in points. Make a list of signs that would tell you you're on the wrong path, and commit to reassessing if those occur. For example, publishing lots of papers in top journals is key to success in academic careers, so you could commit to reassessing the academic path if you don't publish a certain number of papers by the end of your PhD.

---

[50] 80000hours.org/annual-career-review

[51] 80000hours.org/2012/10/sunk-costs-in-careers

Apply this to your own career

Write out your plan using the format above. We've made a tool to help. It checks you've applied all the key ideas we've covered. Take a look here:

http://80k.link/HWC

If you don't have time right now, schedule an afternoon to work through it.

The bottom line: how to make your career plan

You can make a flexible plan by using the A/B/Z method:

- Plan A is the top option you'd like to pursue. If you're relatively confident about what you want to do in the medium-term, focus on that. If you're more uncertain, look to try out several options. If you're very uncertain, plan to do more research while building flexible career capital.
- Plan Bs are the nearby alternatives you can switch into if Plan A doesn't quite go as intended.
- Plan Z is your temporary fallback in case everything goes wrong. Having a Plan Z helps you take bigger risks.

Review your plan at least once a year – you can use the tool on our website:
80000hours.org/annual-career-review

CHAPTER 8

How to find a job

When it comes to advice on how to get a job, most of it is awful.

- CollegeFeed suggests that you "be confident" as their first interview tip, which is a bit like suggesting that you should "be employable".
- Many advisers cover the "clean your nails and have a firm handshake" kind of thing.
- A coach on AOL says that "you need business cards in your pocket at all times." Which is great advice for job

applicants who are so qualified that strangers at parties want to hire them, if only they had their email address.

- A career expert in TIME magazine advises that "By writing blog posts and updating your social status routinely, recruiters will find you when they are looking to hire for a position. As long as your profiles are connected to what you're passionate about, you will attract the right jobs and repel the wrong ones."

So post on Twitter a lot and you'll magically attract the right jobs, right?

Over the last five years, we've sifted through this bad advice to find the nuggets that are actually good. We've also provided one-on-one coaching to hundreds of people who are applying for jobs, and we've hired about 20 people ourselves, so we've seen what works from both sides. Here, we'll sum up what we've learned.

Let's be blunt. You're not entitled to a job, and hiring is rarely fair. Rather, getting a job is, at root, a sales process. You need to persuade someone to give you responsibility and a salary, and even put their reputation on the line, in exchange for results.

We'll list key advice for each stage of the "sales" process: (i) finding opportunities (leads), (ii) convincing employers (conversion), and (iii) negotiating. The common theme is to think from the employer's point of view, and do what they will find most convincing.

While the rest of this guide is about working out which job is best for you and the world, here we focus on the practicalities of taking action on your plans. Just bear in mind there's no point using salesmanship to land a job that you wouldn't be good at – you won't be satisfied, and if your performance is worse than the next best applicant, you'll have a negative impact.

We wrote this chapter to prevent the opposite situation: we've seen too many great candidates who want to make a difference failing to live up to their potential because they don't know how to sell themselves.

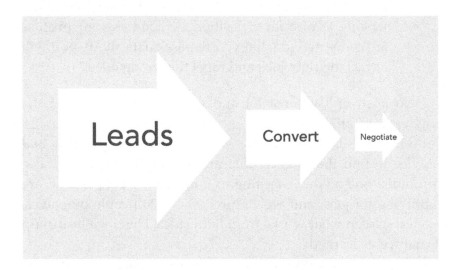

Stage 1: Leads

A lead is any opportunity that might turn into a job, like a position you could apply for, a friend who might know an opportunity, or a side project you might be able to get paid for.

You need lots of leads

We interviewed someone who's now a top *NPR* journalist. But when he started out, he applied to *70* positions and received only one offer that paid over $10,000.

This illustrates the first thing to know about leads: *you probably need a lot of them.* It usually takes 20 to 100 to find one good job, and getting rejected 20 times is normal. In fact, the average length of a spell of unemployment in the US as of

February 2016 is seven months, so be prepared for your job hunt to take that long.

However, there's much you can do to raise your chances of success, which is what we'll now cover.

How to get leads: Don't just send your CV in response to job listings, use connections

Many large organizations have a standardized application process, e.g. the Civil Service, consulting and Teach for America. They want to keep the process fair, so there isn't much wiggle room. In these cases, just apply.

But what do you do after that? The most obvious approach is to send your CV to lots of companies and apply to the postings on job boards. This is often the first thing career advice mentions.

The problem is that sending out your CV and responding to lots of internet job ads has a low success rate. The author of the bestselling career advice book of all time, Dick Bolles, estimates that the chance of landing a job from just sending your resume to a company is around 1 in 1,000. That means you need to send out one hundred resumes just to have a 10% chance of landing a job. This is because once an opportunity is on a job board, it'll be flooded with applicants.

Moreover, the positions on job boards need to be standardized and are mainly at large companies, so they don't include many of the best positions.

The best opportunities are less competitive because they are hidden away, often at small but rapidly growing companies, and personalized to you. You need a different way to find them.

The key is to find leads in the way that employers most like. Employers prefer to hire people they already know, or failing that, to hire through *referrals* – an introduction from someone they know.

Think about it from their point of view. Which would you prefer: a recommendation from someone you trust, or 20 CVs from people who saw your job listing on indeed.com? The referral is more likely to work, because the person has already been vouched for. It's also less effort – screening 20 people you know nothing about is hard. Referrals also come from a better pool of applicants – the most employable people already have lots of offers, so they rarely respond to job listings.

For these reasons, many recruiters consider referrals to be the best method of finding candidates.

But job seekers usually get things backwards – they start with the methods that recruiters *least* like.

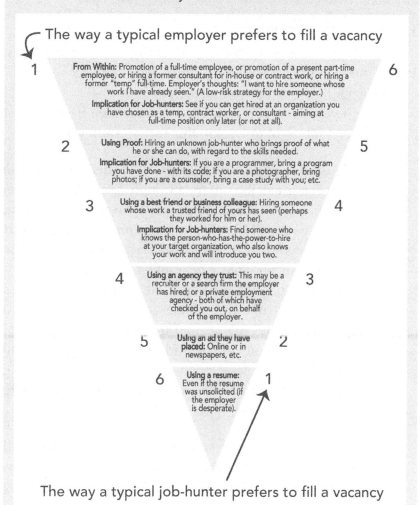

Many if not most employers hunt for job-hunters in the exact opposit way from how most job-hunters hunt for them

The way a typical employer prefers to fill a vacancy

1   **From Within:** Promotion of a full-time employee, or promotion of a present part-time employee, or hiring a former consultant for in-house or contract work, or hiring a former "temp" full-time. Employer's thoughts: "I want to hire someone whose work I have already seen." (A low-risk strategy for the employer.)   6

Implication for Job-hunters: See if you can get hired at an organization you have chosen as a temp, contract worker, or consultant - aiming at full-time position only later (or not at all).

2   **Using Proof:** Hiring an unknown job-hunter who brings proof of what he or she can do, with regard to the skills needed.   5

Implication for Job-hunters: If you are a programmer, bring a program you have done - with its code; if you are a photographer, bring photos; if you are a counselor, bring a case study with you; etc.

3   **Using a best friend or business colleague:** Hiring someone whose work a trusted friend of yours has seen (perhaps they worked for him or her).   4

Implication for Job-hunters: Find someone who knows the person-who-has-the-power-to-hire at your target organization, who also knows your work and will introduce you two.

4   **Using an agency they trust:** This may be a recruiter or a search firm the employer has hired; or a private employment agency - both of which have checked you out, on behalf of the employer.   3

5   **Using an ad they have placed:** Online or in newspapers, etc.   2

6   **Using a resume:** Even if the resume was unsolicited (if the employer is desperate).   1

The way a typical job-hunter prefers to fill a vacancy

What Color is Your Parachute, by Dick Bolles, 2015 ed.

Moreover, applicants find around 50% of jobs through connections, and many are never advertised.[52] So if you don't pursue referrals, you'll miss many opportunities.

How to get referrals

You need to master the art of asking for introductions. We've put together a list of email scripts you can use:

80000hours.org/articles/email-scripts.

To get referrals, here's a step-by-step process. If you're not applying for a job right now, skip this section until you are.

1. **First, update your LinkedIn profile.** This isn't because you'll get great job offers through LinkedIn – that's pretty rare – it's because people who are considering meeting you will check out your profile. Focus your profile on your most impressive accomplishments. Be as concrete as possible, e.g. "ranked third in the nation", "increased annual donations 100%". Cut the rest. It's better to have two impressive achievements than two impressive achievements and three weak ones. Finally, search yourself on Google and do anything you can to make the results look good (e.g. delete embarrassing old blog posts). Follow the link in the footnote for more advice.[53]

2. If you **already know someone in the industry well who can hire people, then ask for a meeting** to discuss opportunities in the industry. This is close to going

---

[52] 80000hours.org/2013/05/how-important-is-networking-for-career-success

[53] There's a guide at lifehacker.com/5963864/how-to-clean-up-your-online-presence-and-make-a-great-first-impression.

directly to an interview, skipping all the screening steps. Remember, there doesn't need to be an open position – employers will often create positions for good people. Before you take the meeting, use the advice on how to prepare for interviews below.

3. If you know them less well, ask for a meeting to find out more about jobs in the industry: an **"informational interview"**. If it goes well, ask them to introduce you to people who may be able to hire you, which is effectively getting a referral from this person. **Do not ask them** for a job if you promised it was an informational interview.

4. When asking for more introductions, **prepare a one-sentence, specific description of the types of opportunities you'd like to find.** A good example is something like: "an entry-level marketing position at a technology startup in education". Two bad examples are: "a job in software" or "a job that fits my skills". Being clear and specific makes it easier for people to come up with ideas, so lean towards too narrow rather than too broad.

5. Failing the above steps, **turn to the connections of your connections.** If you have a good friend who knows someone who's able to hire you, then you could directly ask that friend for a referral. The ideal is to ask someone you've worked for before where you performed really well.

6. If your connection is not able to refer you, then ask them to introduce you to people in the industry who *are* able to hire. Then we're back to informational interviews as in step two.

7. To find out who your connections know, use LinkedIn. Say you want to work at Airbnb. Go to LinkedIn and search "Airbnb". It'll show a list of all your contacts who work at Airbnb, followed by connections of connections who work at Airbnb. Pick the person with the most mutual connections and get in touch.

8. Remember, if you have 200 LinkedIn connections, and each of them has 200 connections that don't overlap with the others, then you can reach at least 10,000 people using these methods.

9. There are lots of people in the 80,000 Hours LinkedIn group (linkedin.com/groups/5057625) who are happy to give advice on applications, and may be able to make introductions.

10. If you still haven't got anywhere, then it may be worth spending some time building your connections in the industry first.[54] Start with people with whom you have some connection, such as your university alumni, and friends of friends of friends (3rd order connections). Your university can probably give you a list of alumni who are willing to help in each industry. There are probably some good groups you can join and conferences to attend. Otherwise you can resort to cold-emailing.[55]

---

[54] We have advice on how to network at 80000hours.org/2015/03/how-to-network.

[55] For a guide to getting jobs with no connections, see cultivatedculture.com/how-to-get-a-job-anywhere-no-connections. For a guide to getting anyone's email address, see life-longlearner.com/find-email-addresses.

Recruiters and listings

We prefer the above tactics, but recruiters can be worth talking to, and are often more effective than just making applications. Look for those who have a good network in the industry you're interested in. If you want to work in an organization with a social purpose, check out ReWork (rework.jobs). There are also recruiters who specialize in new graduates, e.g. GradQuiz in the UK (gradquiz.com).

In case you want to browse job listings, which does sometimes work, and can be a useful way to get ideas, here are some of the main sites:

- Indeed.com aggregates job listings from across the web.
- If you're interested in professional jobs in the US, check out The Muse (themuse.com/jobs) and The Ladders (theladders.com).
- Your university probably has a job listing site targeted to graduates of your university.
- There are listing sites that specialize in certain sectors e.g. Idealist.org specializes in non-profit sector jobs, Angel List (angel.co/jobs) specializes in startup jobs, and internships.com specializes in internships.

Stage 2: Conversion

When you're in contact with someone who has the power to hire you, how do you convince them?

Again, think about it from their point of view. Once at 80,000 Hours, we were trying to hire a web engineer. Most applicants just filled out our application form, while one sent us a redesigned version of our career quiz. Which application is more convincing? The person who sent the quiz was immediately in the top 20% of applicants, despite having very little formal experience.

Employers are looking for several qualities. They want employees who will fit in socially, stick around and not cause trouble. But most importantly, the employer wants to be sure that you can solve the problems they face. If you can prove that you'll get the results the employer most values, everything else is much less important.

So how can you go about doing that?

When the process is highly standardized

In these cases, you have to jump through the hoops. Maximize your chances by finding out exactly what the process involves, and practicing exactly that. For instance, if it's a competency interview, find out which competencies they look for, then have a friend ask you similar questions. Some public service organizations publish the rubrics they use to assess candidates.

The most useful thing you can do is find someone who recently went through the process, ask them how it works, and, if possible, practice the key steps with them. Sometimes there are books written about exactly how to apply.

Most employers, however, don't have a fully standardized process. What do you do in those cases?

If you've already done the same work before, then you just need to practice telling your story. Skip ahead to the interview tips. But what about if you don't have much relevant experience?

The basic idea is: *do free work.*

Do free work

The most powerful way to prove you can do the work is to actually do some of it. And as we saw in Chapter 6, doing the work is the best way to figure out whether you're good at it, so it'll help you to avoid wasting your own time too.

Here are three ways to put that into practice.

The pre-interview project

This is what the web engineer did with our career quiz.

1. Find out what you'd be doing in the role (this already puts you quite a way ahead).
2. In particular, work out which problems you will need to solve for the organization. To figure this out, you'll probably need to do some desk research[56] then speak to people in the industry.
3. Spend a weekend putting together a solution to these problems, and send them to a couple of people at the company with an invitation to talk more.
4. If you don't hear back after a week, follow up at least once.
5. Alternatively, write up your suggestions, and present them during the interview. Ramit Sethi calls this "the briefcase technique".

Speaking from personal experience, we've overseen four years' worth of competitive application processes at the Centre for Effective Altruism, and doing this would immediately put you in the top 20% of applicants, even if your suggestions

---

[56] There is a simple guide to this at themuse.com/advice/the-ultimate-guide-to-researching-a-company-preinterview.

weren't that good. It demonstrates a lot of enthusiasm, and most people hardly know anything about the role they are applying for.

Trial period

If the employer is on the fence, you can offer to do a two to four-week trial period, perhaps at reduced pay or as an intern. Say that you're keen to work there and feel confident that you'll work out. Make it clear that if the employer isn't happy at the end, you'll leave gracefully.

Only bring this out if the employer is on the fence, or it can seem like you're underselling yourself.

Go for a nearby position

If you can't get the job you want right away, consider applying for another position in the organization – like a freelance position, or a position one step below the one you really want. Working in a nearby position gives you the opportunity to prove your motivation and cultural fit. When your boss has a position to fill, it's much easier to promote someone he or she already worked with than to start a lengthy application process.

How to prepare for interviews

If you can *show* the employer you can solve their problems, you're most of the way there, and you can ignore most of the interview advice out there. However, you won't always have time to show, and there's more you can do to become even more convincing.

Here's the best advice we've found on preparing for interviews. It's also useful for getting leads while networking. If you're not actively looking for a job right now, skip this section for now.

1. **When you meet an employer, ask lots of questions to understand their challenges.** Discuss how you might be able to contribute to solving these challenges. This is exactly what great salespeople do. A survey of research on sales in *SPIN Selling* by Neil Rackman, concluded "there is a clear statistical association between the use of questions and the success of the interaction." Moreover, when salespeople were trained to ask more questions, it made them more effective.

2. **Prepare your three key selling points ahead of meetings.** These are the messages you'll try to get in during the discussion. For instance: 1) I have done this work successfully before, 2) I am really excited about this company, 3) I have suggestions for what I could work on. Writing these out ahead of time makes it more likely you'll mention what's most important, and three points is about the limit of what your audience will remember. That's why this is standard advice when pitching a business idea. If you're not sure what you have to offer, there's an exercise at the end of Chapter 5 to inventory your career capital.

3. **Focus on what's most impressive.** What sounds better: "I advised Obama on energy policy" or "I advised Obama on energy policy, and have worked as a high school teacher the last three years"? Many people fill up their CVs with everything they've done, but it's usually better to pick your one or two most impressive achievements and focus on those. It sounds better, it makes it more likely you'll cover it, and it makes it more likely your audience will remember it.

4. **Prepare concrete facts and stories to back up your three key messages.** For instance, if you're applying to be a web engineer, rather than "I'm a hard-worker", try "I have a friend who runs an organization that was about to get some press coverage. He needed to build a website in 24 hours, so we pulled an all-nighter to build it. The next day we got 1,000 sign-ups." Rather than say "I really want to work in this industry", tell the story of what led you to apply. Stories and concrete details are far more memorable than abstract claims.

5. **Work out how to sum up what you have to offer in a sentence.** Steve Jobs didn't sell millions of iPods by saying they're 30% better than mp3 players, but rather with the slogan "1,000 songs in your pocket". Having a short, vivid summary makes it easy for other people to promote you on your behalf. For instance "He's the guy who advised Obama on climate policy and wants a research position."

6. **Prepare answers to the most likely questions.** Write them out, then practice saying them out loud. The following three questions normally come up: (1) Tell me about yourself – this is an opportunity to tell the story of why you want this position and mention one or two achievements (2) Why do you want this position? (3) What are your questions for us? Then usually the interviewer will add some behavioral questions about the traits they care most about. These usually start "tell me about a time you…", then are finished with things like: "exhibited leadership", "had to work as a team", "had to deal with a difficult situation or person", "you failed", "you succeeded". You can find a list of common

interview questions by following the link in the footnotes.[57]

7. **Practice the meeting, from start to finish.** Meet with a friend and have them ask you five interview questions, then practice responding quickly. If you don't have a friend to help, then say your answers out loud and mentally rehearse how you want it to go. Ask yourself what's most likely to go wrong, and what you'll do if that happens.

8. **Learn.** After each interview, jot down what went well, what could have gone better, and what you'll do differently next time.

To learn more about sales, our top recommendation is *SPIN Selling*, which is based on in-depth research by Neil Rackman.

Stage 3: Negotiation

Negotiation begins after you have an offer, that is, once the employer has said they'd like to hire you.

Most people are so happy to get a job, or awkward about the idea of negotiating, that they never try. But ten minutes of negotiation could mean major benefits over the next couple of years. So, *actually consider doing it.*

For instance, you could ask the employer to match your donations to charity. That could mean thousands of dollars of

---

[57] "How to answer the most common 31 interview questions" on The Muse: https://www.themuse.com/advice/how-to-answer-the-31-most-common-interview-questions

extra donations per year, making those ten minutes you took to negotiate the most productive of your life.

You could also negotiate to work on a certain team, have more flexible hours, work remotely, or learn certain skills. All of these could make a big difference to your day-to-day happiness and career capital.

Negotiation is not *always* appropriate. Don't do it if you've landed a highly standardized offer, like a Civil Service position – they won't be able to change the contract. Also don't do it if you're only narrowly better than the other candidates or have no alternatives. And definitely don't negotiate until the employer has made an offer – it looks really bad to start negotiating during the interview.

However, we think negotiation should be tried in most cases once you have an offer. Hiring someone takes months and consumes lots of management time. Once an employer has made an offer, they've invested many thousands of dollars in the process. The top candidate is often significantly better than the next best. This means it's unlikely that they'll let the top candidate get away for, say, a 5% increase in costs.

It's even more unlikely that they'll retract their initial offer because you tried to negotiate. Stay polite, and the worst case is likely that they'll stick to their original offer.

Negotiation should be most strongly considered when you have more than one good offer, because then you have a strong fallback position.

How to negotiate

Explain the value you'll give the employer, and why it's justified to give you the benefits you want. The idea is to look for objective metrics and win-win solutions – can you give up something the employer cares about in exchange for something you care about? For instance:

164

- I'm going to redesign your sign-up process, increasing the conversion rate by 1%, which is worth millions of dollars to you, so I'd like to be given donation-matching up to $50,000. This is something I value, and the company can claim tax benefits on the donations.

- Other people with my level of experience in this industry are usually paid $50,000 and can work at home two days per week. But I'd prefer to work with you. Can you match the other companies?

- I'm really motivated to learn sales skills, so I'd like to work alongside person X. This will make me much more effective in the role in six months.

A huge amount has been written about salary negotiation, so this hardly scratches the surface.[58]

Negotiate after you've started

Once you start the job, try to perform as well as possible, and then negotiate again. Most employers will be very unwilling to lose someone who's already doing excellent work. Just bear in mind, most companies have a standard review process, so wait until then to make your ask.

---

[58] There's a good guide at kalzumeus.com/2012/01/23/salary-negotiation. If you want to get more advanced, check out the book *Getting Past No* by William Ury, who developed the negotiation course at Harvard Law School.

Stay motivated

The job search may be one of the hardest things you've ever done – you've probably never been rejected 30 times in a row before. And you may have to do most of it alone. It makes online dating look easy.

This means that you'll need to throw every motivational technique you know at the job hunt. For example, set a really specific goal like speaking to five people each week until you have an offer, publicly commit to the goal, and promise to make a forfeit if you miss it. We know one job seeker who, although he is liberal, promised to donate to the Trump campaign if he missed his goal.

One of the most useful approaches our members have found is pairing up with someone else who is also job hunting. Check in on progress, and share tips and leads. Alternatively, find someone who was recently successful at a similar hunt and is willing to meet up and give you tips.

To get more practical tips on how to motivate yourself, check out the book *The Motivation Hacker* by Nick Winter.

Check out our advice on different jobs

The best way to get a job depends on the type of job you're pursuing. Go to the career profiles at the end of this book, and find the full version online. Many of the reviews contain step-by-step advice on how to enter.

Never job hunt again

Your job hunts will get easier and easier as you build career capital.

The most important thing you can do to put yourself in a better position is gain more connections, so you can get better referrals. We have tips on that in section 5 of Appendix 2, and in the next chapter.

Also focus on developing strong skills and really kicking ass in your work. The best marketing is word of mouth – employers seeking you out rather than the other way around. If you're great at your job, then people will actively want to refer you to employers, because it's doing them a favor as well as you.

Conclusion

Getting a job can be an unpleasant process, but if you go through the steps in this chapter, you'll give yourself the best chance of success. And that will make sure you fulfil your potential to find a satisfying career and contribute to the world.

Apply this to your own career

What are the most important three steps to take in order to get into your top options?

Try to be as specific as possible. Some good examples: Complete an online course in statistics; follow up with my boss at my last internship; read my top-recommended problem profile. The key steps probably involve speaking to people.

When are you going to do each of these? Many studies have shown that writing down *when* you'll do a task makes it much more likely you'll actually do it – it's called an "implementation intention".

The bottom line: how to find a job

- Getting a job is a sales process. Think of it from the employer's point of view, and do what the employer will find most convincing.

- Get lots of leads, especially by asking for introductions.

- Prove you can do the work by actually doing it. Do a project before the interview, explain exactly how you can solve their problems or seek a related position first.

- Once you get an offer, actually negotiate.

- Do whatever it takes to keep yourself motivated, e.g. make a public commitment to apply for one position per day or find a partner to search for jobs alongside.

CHAPTER 9

Why community is key

Everyone knows that networking is important for a good career, but what people don't tell you is that there's something even more important: community.

If you become a valued member of a community, you'll gain hundreds of connections at once, because once one person vouches for you, they can introduce you to everyone else. That means it's like networking but a hundred times more effective.

In fact, getting involved in a good community is perhaps the single biggest thing you can do to help your career.

Introducing our community

There are lots of great communities out there, but there's one we want to highlight in particular: the effective altruism community.

It's a group of people devoted to using evidence and reason to figure out the most effective ways to help others, using the ideas in this guide.

We helped to start the community back in 2012, along with several other groups. There are now over 100 meet-ups around the world and around 20 conferences every year, including one in Asia and one in Africa. Most importantly, the community gets stuff done - its members have pledged billions of dollars to effective charities and founded over 10 organizations focused on doing good.

If you liked this guide, then you'll probably like lots of people in this community. But the real reason we're highlighting it is because it helps people to have a much greater impact.

Why get involved?

We've seen people get all kinds of help and advice, become more altruistic and ambitious, change how they think about doing good, and achieve far more than they ever expected.

For instance, Ilan founded a non-profit in his second year at university, which now has an annual budget of over $300,000. He met mentors and donors through the community.

Another member, Sam, donated hundreds of thousands of dollars to charity before he turned 26. He was helped by someone in the community who told him about an internship. They were happy to advise because they knew Sam was planning to give away a large share of his income.

We know people who have been involved with McKinsey, Harvard Business School, the Fulbright scholarship, the World Economic Forum, and other prestigious networks, but many of them say they find it more useful to meet other people in the effective altruism community.

In a normal network, people are pursuing their own projects, so it's hard to collaborate.

However, in the effective altruism community, everyone shares the same goal: to help others as much as possible. If you help someone else to have a greater impact, then you increase your own impact too, so you both succeed.

In the end, we can achieve far more if we work together. People have complementary strengths and weaknesses – a designer and an engineer can together build a much better product than either could alone. So ten people working together can achieve far more than ten people working separately.

In the early days of 80,000 Hours, there were two people who had to choose between running the organization and earning to give. We realized that Ben would be better at the former and the other had higher earning potential. So, Ben became the CEO, and the other person became our first major donor, enabling us to grow much faster than we could have otherwise.

A group of people can also explore more widely than an individual, identifying better ways to contribute. For instance, Dr. Greg Lewis did the research into how many lives a doctor saves that we saw earlier. After realizing it was less than he thought, he decided not to focus on clinical medicine. Now, he's studying public health with the aim of becoming an expert on the topic within the community. By doing that, he can help the rest of the community become more effective.

In fact, even if we *don't* share a common goal, we can achieve more by working together. Suppose you run an animal rights charity and meet someone who runs a global health charity. You don't think global health is a pressing problem, and the other person doesn't think animal rights is a pressing problem, so neither of you think the other's charity has much impact. But suppose you know a donor who might give to their charity, and they know a donor who might give to your charity. You can trade: if you both make introductions, which is a small cost, you might both find a new donor, which is a big benefit.

How can we work together more effectively?

There's a lot to say about how best to coordinate. If you're already involved in the community, read our articles on "talent gaps" and the "value of coordination".[59]

How to get involved

If you're new, read *Doing Good Better*

Doing Good Better is a book by our co-founder Will MacAskill about effective altruism. Steven Levitt, author of Freakonomics, said it "should be required reading for anyone interested in making the world better" so you know it's got to be good.

Then join the newsletter

If you've already read the book, join the effective altruism monthly newsletter. It'll keep you up to date about new discoveries and important events in the community.

www.effectivealtruism.org/get-involved

---

[59] 80000hours.org/2015/11/why-you-should-focus-more-on-talent-gaps-not-funding-gaps

80000hours.org/2016/02/the-value-of-coordination

If you already know the basics, meet the local community

Meet other people trying to make a difference in our LinkedIn group, by searching Facebook for a local group (e.g. "effective altruism London"), and by attending an "Effective Altruism Global" conference near you. Once you've met a few people in the community, ask for introductions to the types of people you'd most like to speak to.

Start by aiming to meet people in a similar situation to yourself, since there will often be opportunities to help each other. Then, try to speak to people who are one or two steps ahead of you (e.g. if you want to start an organization, meet people who started one last year).

When you're getting involved, look for "five minute favors" – quick ways you can help someone else in the community. There are probably some small things you can do that will be a great help to someone else in the community, and if you build a reputation for being helpful, other people will want to help you back. See more tips on networking in section 5 of Appendix 2.

Finally, look for projects you could contribute to – the people who get the most out of the community are those who make the largest contribution.

Start now by joining our LinkedIn group. You can ask questions about your career, see high-impact job openings, and find people in the industries you want to enter by searching the group:

www.linkedin.com/groups/5057625

A final word

Before we end, imagine that you're at the end of your 80,000 hour career. You're on your deathbed looking back.

What are some things you might regret?

Perhaps you drifted into whatever seemed like the easiest option, or did what your parents did.

Maybe you even made a lot of money doing something you were interested in, and had a nice house and car. But you still wonder: what was it all for?

Now imagine instead that you worked really hard throughout your life, and ended up saving the lives of a hundred children. Can you really imagine regretting that?

To have a truly fulfilling life, we need to turn outwards rather than inwards. Rather than asking, "what would most make me passionate?", ask "how can I best contribute to the world?".

And as we've seen, by using our fortunate position, and acting strategically, there's a huge amount we can all do.

The entire guide, in brief

To have a good career, focus on the following, roughly in this order:

1. **Explore** to find the best options, rather than "going with your gut" or narrowing down too early. Make

this your key focus until you become more confident about the best options.

2. Take the best opportunities to **invest in your career capital** to become as badass as you can be. Especially look for career capital that's flexible when you're uncertain.

3. **Help others** by focusing on the most pressing social problems rather than those you stumble into – those that are big in scale, neglected and solvable. To make the largest contribution to those problems, consider earning to give, research and advocacy, as well as direct work.

4. **Keep adapting your plan to find the best personal fit.** Rather than expect to discover your "passion" right away, think like a scientist testing a hypothesis.

5. And work with a **community**.

By working together, in our lifetimes, we can end extreme global poverty and factory farming, we can prevent climate change and safeguard the future, and we can do this while having interesting, fulfilling lives too. So let's do it.

You have 80,000 hours in your career.

Don't waste them.

What now?

If you still need to make a career plan, try out our tool: **http://80k.link/HWC**

If you already have a plan, start to take action by meeting people in our community, using the steps in the previous section.

If you've found this guide useful, and know someone else in the midst of planning their career, we've created a simple tool to give them a free copy:
80000hours.org/gift

Or, if you'd like to share the guide more broadly, you can do so here:
80000hours.org/share

The rest of this book

As you may have noticed, you're not at the end quite yet. In the rest of the book, we include:

- A short summary of our key ideas.
- Some additional articles that further explore key ideas.
- Summaries of our top career reviews.
- Summaries of our problem area profiles.

If you'd like more reading after that (we admire your stamina!), please see a list of everything on our website, including our advanced content:
http://80k.link/VOF

Summary of key ideas

Job satisfaction

The following are key ingredients for a dream job:

1. Work you're good at,

2. Work that helps others, i.e. that makes a large contribution to a pressing problem.

3. Supportive conditions:
   a. Engaging work that lets you enter a state of flow,
   b. Supportive colleagues,
   c. A job that meets your basic needs, like fair pay, a short commute and reasonable hours, and
   d. A job that fits your personal life.

Making a difference

The difference you make is the number of lives you improve and how much you improve them by.

Any college grad in the developed world can make a major difference to the lives of hundreds of people. They can do this by donating 10% of their income to the world's poorest people;

using their political influence, such as by voting; or by helping others have a greater impact.

The most pressing problems

To find the most pressing problems, look for those that are:

- Large in scale,
- Unfairly neglected,
- Solvable and
- In an area with which you have personal fit.

Which careers most help others?

- First, focus on the most pressing problem areas.

- Then, work out how you can make the biggest contribution to those problems.

- The more pressing the problem and the bigger the contribution, the larger the impact.

- To have a large contribution, consider indirect approaches such as research, advocacy and earning to give, as well as direct work. You might be able to find a path that offers more influence, that's a better fit for the problem, or that's a better fit for you.

- Finally, because the most successful careers in a field achieve far more than the typical one, choose something where you have the potential to excel. The best option is the one with the best balance of personal fit and general potential for impact.

Career capital

- Career capital is anything that puts you in a better position to make a difference in the future, including skills, connections, credentials, and savings.

- Gaining career capital is important throughout your career, but especially when you're young and you have a lot to learn.

- The earlier you are in your career, and the less certain you are about what to do in the medium-term, the more you should focus on gaining career capital that's *flexible*, i.e. useful in many different industries and career paths.

The right career for you

- It's really hard to work out what you're going to be good at ahead of time, especially just by "going with your gut".

- So instead, *go investigate*. After an initial cut-down of your options, go learn more and then try them out.

- Minimize the costs of trying out your options by trying things in the best order (e.g. corporate sector before non-profit sector.

- Keep adapting your plan over time. Think like a scientist investigating a hypothesis.

Career planning

You can make a flexible plan by using the A/B/Z method:

- Plan A is the top option you'd like to pursue.
    - o If you're relatively confident about what you want to do in the medium-term, focus on how to get into that option as quickly as possible.
    - o If you're more uncertain, look to try out several options over a couple of years.
    - o If you're very uncertain, make a plan to do more research while building flexible career capital.

- Plan Bs are the nearby alternatives you can switch into if Plan A doesn't quite go as intended.

- Plan Z is your temporary fallback in case everything goes wrong. Having a Plan Z helps you take bigger risks.

Review your plan at least once a year, because you won't be right first time, and the situation will change.

How to get a job

- Get lots of leads, especially by asking for introductions.

- Prove you can do the work by actually doing it. Do a project before the interview, explain exactly how you can solve their problems or seek a related position first.

- Once you get an offer, negotiate.

- Do whatever it takes to keep yourself motivated, e.g. make a public commitment to apply for one position per day or find a partner to search for jobs alongside.

APPENDIX 1

The meaning of making a difference

Definition

We define "making a difference" or "having a social impact" as follows:

The number of people whose lives you improve, and how much you improve them by.

We think of "improving lives" in terms of "increasing wellbeing" or "increasing flourishing". We think everyone is equally valuable, and we think it's reasonable to extend "people" to include non-humans.

The role of value judgements

The exact meaning of "flourishing lives" is a value judgement. Most people agree about the basics (torture is bad, health is good), but some important issues are up for debate, and these can affect what the phrase "making a difference" means to you. For instance, the more highly you weigh the interests of animals compared to humans, the more you'll care about ending factory farming compared to other problems.

Fortunately, most of our advice doesn't depend on a particular definition of flourishing lives. Different values will lead individuals to different conclusions about which problems are most pressing. However, things like acquiring career capital, maintaining career flexibility, building influence, and correctly weighing your options are largely independent of value judgments and useful to almost everyone. So we can help people contribute to solving a variety of problems, depending on their values.

Moreover, even when it comes to the question of which problems are most pressing, the main disagreements are often empirical rather than about values.

When our advice *does* depend on value judgements, we try to explicitly flag it so that you can make up your own mind. For instance, rather than present a single list of pressing problems, we made a quiz that leads you through some of the most important judgement calls (80000hours.org/problem-quiz).

How do you measure impact in practice?

In practical terms, we think of your impact as the extent to which you contribute to solving social problems faster than they would have been solved otherwise.

This means you have a larger impact when (i) the problem is larger and (ii) you make a larger counterfactual contribution to it.

How can you actually compare the scale of different social problems, given that in practice they're extremely hard to measure?

Being difficult to measure doesn't mean comparisons are impossible, it just means that we need to use approximate heuristics or 'yardsticks' instead. For instance, you can compare problems in terms of how much they increase wealth, health, long-run security, and other important goals. (You can see the rubric we use to assess the scale of different problems at 80000hours.org/articles/problem-framework.)

When we're uncertain we also use probabilities. For instance, a 90% chance of helping 100 people is roughly equivalent to a 100% chance of helping 90 people.

In practice, we recommend focusing on the problems that are most pressing according to our framework, and going into the careers where you can gain the greatest influence to solve these problems.

Why 'faster than they would have been solved otherwise'?

The true impact of an action depends on what happens *because of that action*, not on what happens, period. When we work hard and see positive results, it's often easy to neglect the

80,000 Hours

fact that some portion of those results would have occurred anyway, or that someone else might have filled our role just as well as we did. There is often a gap between true impact and 'tangible impact' – the immediate results of our actions – and understanding that gap is crucial to finding the places where you can make a real difference.

What about justice and the environment?

Our definition of social impact is about helping people (and perhaps animals) live better lives. People sometimes wonder whether this means we don't care about other values like justice, equality, or the environment.

There are a few things to say about this:

1. We do care about advancing justice, because a more just world is one in which people will live better lives, i.e. advancing justice has social impact. Similarly, we care about the environment, because we need the environment so that humans and animals can live better lives.

2. Justice and other values may well matter independently of their effect on people. However, this isn't our focus. We focus on helping people live good lives, and only look to advance justice insofar as it helps with that. We chose flourishing as the key thing to focus on because it's something that almost everyone thinks is important, while there's also a huge difference in the effect of different careers on the amount of flourishing in the

186

world. This means everyone should agree it's a really important aim to focus on.

3. Even if you don't care that much about flourishing compared to these other values, you can still use our advice. You'll just have a different ranking of problems from us. The rest of our advice remains nearly unchanged.

APPENDIX 2

Eleven ways to put yourself in a better position in any job

You can gain valuable skills, connections and credentials – what we call career capital – by both choosing the right jobs, and doing the right things within your current role.

Here's a list of the best ways we've found to improve your career capital in any job.

We recommend working on one at a time, so skim through the list then pick one area to work on. They're roughly in order: apply the earlier advice first, then move on to the more advanced tips. Generally, the earlier tips are useful in a wider range of situations, have bigger effects and are quicker to apply.

1. Look after yourself, and take care of the basics

The basics are getting enough sleep, exercising, eating right and maintaining your closest friendships. All of these make a big difference to your energy and productivity, and prevent you from burning out. They also do a lot to drive how happy you feel day to day (probably much more than other factors people tend to focus on, like income).

So if there's anything you can do to significantly improve one of these areas, it's worth taking care of it first. A lot has been written about how to improve each of these areas by building better habits. A good starting point is the list at alexvermeer.com/life-hacking.

2. Look after your mental health

About 20% of people in their twenties have some kind of mental health problem, and depression is much more common among the young than the old.

If you're suffering from a mental health issue – be it anxiety, bipolar disorder, depression or something else – then make dealing with it or learning to cope your top priority. It is one of the best investments you can ever make both for your own sake and your ability to help others. We know people who took the time to focus intensely on dealing with serious mental health problems and who, having found treatments and techniques that worked, have gone on to perform at the highest level.

Mental health is not our area of expertise, and we can't offer medical advice. We'd recommend seeking professional help as your first step. If you're at university, there should be free services available.

Cognitive behavioral therapy (CBT) has also been found to help with many mental health problems, and is increasingly available online. One resource to check out is Go Lantern (golantern.com).

The UK's national health service publishes useful, evidence-based advice[60] and there are some excellent resources for depression, anxiety and ADHD.[61]

All the same applies if you have a problem with your physical health – look after your health first.

3. Take advantage of positive psychology

There have been plenty of recent discoveries about the sources of wellbeing (as we mentioned in Chapter 1). Besides taking care of sleep, exercise, diet and friendships, positive psychologists have developed exercises designed to help you be happier, and tested them with randomized controlled trials. It seems well worth trying out these exercises as a way to prevent burnout, protect your mental health, perform better, and hell, just to enjoy your life more.

Here's a list of techniques recommended by Professor Martin Seligman, one of the founders of the field. Most of these are in his book, *Flourish*.

---

[60] See www.nhs.uk/Livewell/mentalhealth/Pages/Mentalhealthhome.aspx.

[61] For depression: slatestarcodex.com/2014/06/16/things-that-sometimes-help-if-youre-depressed

For anxiety: slatestarcodex.com/2015/07/13/things-that-sometimes-work-if-you-have-anxiety

For ADHD consider "Cognitive-Behavioural Therapy for Adult ADHD: Targeting Executive Dysfunction" by Mary Solanto and "Taking Charge of Adult ADHD" by Russell Barkley.

1. Rate your happiness at the end of each day. You'll become more self-aware and be able to track your progress over time. Moodscope (moodscope.com) is a good tool.

2. Gratitude journaling – write down three things you're grateful for at the end of each day, and why they happened. Other ways of cultivating gratitude are also good, like the gratitude visit.

3. Using your signature strengths. Take the VIA Sig Strengths survey.[62] Then make sure you use one of your top five strengths each day.

4. Learn basic cognitive behavioral therapy. A simple exercise is the ABCD which you could do at the end of each day.

5. Mindfulness practice – usually done via meditation. We recommend Headspace (headspace.com) and the book, *Mindfulness* by Penman and Williams.

6. Do something kind each day, like donating to charity, giving someone a compliment, or helping someone at work.

7. Practice active constructive responding.[63]

8. Adopt the growth mindset. If you believe you can improve your abilities, you'll be more resilient to failure

---

[62] viacharacter.org/www/The-Survey

[63] gostrengths.com/what-is-active-and-constructive-responding

and harder working. See the excellent book, *Mindset*, by Carol Dweck, which reviews this research and discusses how the mindset can be learned.

To get more exercises, read *The How of Happiness* by Sonja Lyubomirsky.

4. Save money

We recommend saving enough money that you could comfortably live for at least six months if you had no income, and ideally twelve. First, it gives you security; second it gives you the flexibility to make big career changes. The standard advice is also to save about 15% of your income for retirement.

How to save money?

- Save automatically. Set up a direct debit from your main account to a savings account, so you never notice the money.

- Focus on big wins. Rather than constantly scrimping (don't buy that latte!), identify one or two areas of your budget you could cut that will have a big effect. Often cutting rent by moving somewhere smaller or sharing a house with someone else is the biggest thing.

- But beware of swapping money for time. Suppose you could save $100 per month by moving somewhere with an hour longer commute. Instead, maybe you could spend that time working overtime, making you more likely to get promoted, or earning extra wages. You'd only need to earn $5/hour to break even with the more expensive rent.

- Until you have six months' runway, cut your donations back to 1%.

- For more tips, check out Mr Money Mustache (mrmoneymustache.com) and Ramit Sethi's book, *I Will Teach You to be Rich*.

Bear in mind that it might be more effective to focus on earning more rather than spending less, especially through negotiating your salary (see Chapter 8).

Once you're saving 15% and have 12 months' runway, move on to the next step.[64]

5. Surround yourself with great people

Why networking is more important than you think

Everyone talks about the importance of your network for a successful career, and they're right. A large fraction of jobs are found through connections and many are probably never advertised, so only available through connections.

But the importance of connections goes far beyond finding jobs. It may be an overstatement to say that "you become the average of the five people you spend the most time with", but

---

[64] For more reading on personal finance for people who want to donate to charity, see an introductory guide at benkuhn.net/giving-101 and an advanced guide at reducing-suffering.org/advanced-tips-on-personal-finance.

there is certainly some truth in it. Your friends set the behavior you see as normal (social norms), and directly influence how you feel (through emotional contagion). Your friends can also directly teach you new skills and introduce you to new people.

Researchers have even measured this influence, which is reviewed in the book *Connected* by Christakis and Fowler. One study found that if one of your friends becomes more happy, you're 15% more likely to be happy. If a friend of a friend becomes happy, you're 10% more likely to be happy; and if a friend of a friend of a friend becomes happy, you're still 6% more likely to be happy. The researchers don't think this effect is caused by the fact that happy people tend to hang out with other happy people – they used a couple of smart techniques to separate causation from correlation. Negative behaviors like smoking spread in a similar way. Our guess is that who you spend time with is a major factor in your personal growth and character.

Your connections are also a major source of personalized, up-to-date information that is never published. For instance, if you want to find out what job opportunities might be a good fit for you in the biotech industry, the best way to find out is to speak to a friend in that industry. The same is true if you want to learn about the trends in a sector, or the day-to-day reality of a job.

If you ever want to start a new project or hire someone, your connections are the best place to start, because you already know and trust them.

Finally if you care about social impact, then your connections are even more important, because they're also a platform for advocacy. Partly this is because you can persuade people in your network of important ideas. But it's also because your behavior will help to set the social norms in your network, spreading positive behaviors in the way we just described above. For instance, if you become vegetarian, it seems likely that you can cause more than one other person to become vegetarian. In this way, your influence on your network could be more important than the direct impact of your own behaviors. There's evidence in *Connected* to back up this idea, at least in some cases. The more people in your network, and the more influential they are, the more powerful the effect.

How to network

So how can you build connections? Networking sounds icky, but at its core, it's simple: *meet people you like, and help them out.* If you meet lots of people and find small ways to be useful to them, then when you need a favor, you'll have lots of people to turn to. It's best, however, just to help people with no expectation of reward – that's what the best networkers do and there's evidence that it's what works best.

You don't have to meet people through networking conferences. The best way is to meet people through people you already know – just ask for an introduction and explain why you'd like to meet. Otherwise you can meet people through common interests.

Finally, don't forget that you want both depth and breadth of connections – it's useful to have some allies who know you really well and can help you out in a tough spot, but it's also useful to know people in many different areas so you can find diverse perspectives and opportunities. There's evidence that being the 'bridge' between different groups is useful for getting jobs and being successful.

Try to develop habits that will let you build connections automatically, e.g. join a group that meets regularly, or set aside some of your budget to take one person out to dinner each month.[65]

Many people we've advised have found the biggest single way we helped them was by introducing them to a community of likeminded people who want to have a social impact.

You can join in at:

http://80k.link/QNB

6. Do what you can to become more productive

You can find lots of articles about which skills are most in-demand by employers – is it marketing, programming or data science? But what people don't talk about so often are the skills that are useful in *all* jobs.

One example is productivity. Most people we've worked with find that if they work on it, they can become more productive no matter the task. Here's an example: the Pomodoro technique involves setting a 25-minute timer whenever you need to work on a task, and committing to focusing just on that task for 25 minutes. It's hard to imagine a more simple technique, but many people find it helps them to overcome procrastination and be more focused, making a major difference to how much they can get done each day.

If there are opportunities like this lying around, you should take them before you learn a narrower skill, like marketing, because they'll help you no matter what job you end up in.

---

[65] We have more on how to network at 80000hours.org/2015/03/how-to-network.

Here are some other techniques that many people have found helpful. Work through them one at a time, spending several weeks on each until you've built the new habits.

1. Set up a system to track all your small tasks, like a simplified version of the Getting Things Done system.[66]

2. Do a five-minute review at the end of each day. You can put all kinds of other useful habits into this review, e.g. gratitude journaling, tracking your happiness, thinking about what you learned each day. You can also use it to set your top priority for the next day – many people find it useful to focus on this first (a technique called "eating a frog").

3. Each week, perform a review of your key goals, and plan out the rest of the week. (And the same monthly and annually.)

4. Batch your time, e.g. try to have all your meetings in one or two days, then block out solid stretches of time for focused work; clear your inbox once a week.

5. Build a regular daily routine, which you can then use to complete plenty of other tasks automatically, such as exercise.

6. Use motivation techniques, like Beeminder (beeminder .com). Also check out *The Motivation Hacker* by Nick Winter, and *The Procrastination Equation* by Piers Steel.

---

[66] See hamberg.no/gtd.

7. Set up systems to take care of day-to-day tasks to free up your attention, like eating the same thing for breakfast every day for a month.

8. Block social media during work hours, with a tool like Rescue Time (rescuetime.com) or Self-Control (self controlapp.com).

A huge amount has been written about all of these ideas. Hopefully this gives you an idea of what's out there and some ways to get started. We especially recommend the book *Deep Work* by Cal Newport. When you've spent a few months incorporating some of these habits into your routines, move on to the next step.

7. Learn how to learn

Because technology and the world are changing so fast, being successful requires constantly learning new skills. Moreover, the world seems to be becoming more "winner takes all" and the most successful are becoming more and more dominant in their fields, so having world-class expertise has never been more important, and developing that expertise requires a lot of learning. Finally, the ability to learn quickly and effectively will help you to gain all the other skills you need for good career capital.

Perhaps surprisingly, you can become a lot faster at learning. One example is *spaced repetition*. If you're trying to memorize something, like a word in a foreign language, research shows there's an optimal frequency to review the word. If you use this frequency, you'll be able to memorize the word much faster. There are now tools that will do the revising for you, like Anki (ankisrs.net) for making your own flashcards, and Memrise (memrise.com) for pre-prepared cards.

There are lots more techniques. Our top recommendation in this area is a course on Coursera (coursera.org/learn/learning-how-to-learn), which is now the most viewed MOOC of all time.

When you've learned the basics, go on to learning more narrowly applicable skills, as we cover in the next step.

8. Become more rational

Another example of a skill that's useful in every job, but not usually discussed is rational thinking. Recent research shows that intelligence and rationality are distinct,[67] but rationality is much easier to train.

Being able to think well and make good decisions is especially important if you want to engage with the complex challenges of making the world a better place.

Becoming more rational involves building up better habits of thinking, such as those mentioned in Appendix 3.

The Center for Applied Rationality is using the research on rationality to develop practical training programs, especially for people who want to have an impact, and they usually offer discounts to readers of 80,000 Hours. Learn more at rationality.org.

---

[67] For a summary of some of this research, see:
http://www.nytimes.com/2016/09/18/opinion/sunday/the-difference-between-rationality-and-intelligence.html

9. Teach yourself useful skills

You can self-study on the side in any job, and this is easier than ever before thanks to the huge growth in online courses, like Udacity (udacity.com) and Coursera (coursera.org).

But bear in mind often the quickest way to learn a skill is just to do it, while getting feedback from experts. So rather than learning on the side, look for people who can give you feedback, then incorporate it into your work or side projects.

Here are some skills we'd especially recommend studying on the side, because they're transferable and highly in-demand (besides those listed above).[68] Don't try to learn more than one at a time.

1. Persuasion and negotiation
2. Data analysis
3. Communication (especially writing)
4. Analysis and problem-solving
5. Management
6. Programming

Also consider whether to focus on one main skill, or explore lots of skills. In some areas success is more a matter of being exceptional at one thing, e.g. academic careers mainly depend on the quality of your publications. If you're focused on that kind of area, then just focus on getting good at that one thing. Having one impressive achievement is also usually more

---

[68] The recommendations are partly based on our preliminary analysis, available at
80000hours.org/2016/03/which-skills-make-you-most-employable.

useful for opening doors than several ordinary achievements, so that's also reason to focus.

However, in other areas it's useful to have an unusual combination of skills, and become the best person within that niche. For instance, the creator of *Dilbert*, Scott Adams, attributes his success to being fairly good at telling jokes, drawing cartoons, and knowing about the business world. There are many people better than him on each dimension, but put all three together and he's one of the best in the world.

On the other hand, not all combinations of skills are valuable. We can't give hard and fast advice about which combinations are best, or whether to focus on a single skill compared to a portfolio.

However, one combination that *does* seem valuable is the combination of mathematical and social skills. As technology improves, there's more and more demand for people who can work at the intersection of people and technology. On the other hand, people usually specialize in one or the other, so there's a shortage of people who are good at both. Research by Prof. David Deming at Harvard found that jobs which require both mathematical and social skills were among the fastest growing since 1980.[69]

10. Consider changing city

Industries often cluster in certain areas. Go to Silicon Valley for technology, LA for entertainment, New York for

---

[69]https://web.archive.org/save/https://www.weforum.org/agenda/2016/09/jobs-of-future-and-skills-you-need/

advertising, Boston for academia, London for finance, and so on.

These clusters exist for a reason – if everyone's in the same area it makes communication and progress much faster.

People often recommend that ambitious people move to wherever their industry is clustered. Indeed, in some of these industries, the top jobs only exist in certain locations.

We don't see much reason to doubt this advice, and we've advised several people who saw major boosts to their careers after moving (in fact, we've decided to move 80,000 Hours from Oxford to near San Francisco).

Major pay differences also exist across regions, which are often larger than the differences in cost of living, and you can capture these differences if you're willing to move.

Of course, changing city is costly, especially to your personal life. It takes a long time to build up a network of friends, so this is the main cost to consider. We hope to do more research into the pros and cons of moving in the future.

Finally, note that the effective altruism community is clustered in the following cities (in descending order): San Francisco, London / Oxford / Cambridge, Boston, Berlin, Melbourne, and Vancouver. Visiting one of the major hubs is a good way to meet people in the community, and especially helpful if you're looking for a job.[70]

11. Become an expert and innovator

After you've taken the low-hanging fruit from the steps above, and explored different areas, one end game to consider

---

[70] See effective-altruism.com/ea/hu/should_you_visit_an_ea_hub.

is becoming a recognized leader in a highly valuable skill-set or problem area.

As we covered in Chapter 5, the best research available suggests that expertise in established areas takes 10 to 30 years of focused practice to build, depending on the area. It's debated how important practice is compared to talent, luck and other factors, but everyone agrees that it's necessary in well-established areas. It also seems that most people can improve at most skills with practice, so even if you can't reach expert levels, you can still improve a great deal.

To find out more about this research, and find out how to practice effectively, we recommend reading *Peak* by K. Anders Ericsson (though bear in mind Ericsson is the biggest advocate of practice being important compared to talent). For more practical advice on how to practice within knowledge-work jobs, we recommend *Deep Work* by Cal Newport.

We think it's prudent to focus on an area where you think you might also have talent. To find out where you're most talented, we recommend exploring lots of areas, as we argue in Chapter 6, and seeing *where you improve fastest*. There may be other restrictions to bear in mind, for instance, some fields also seem to require that you start by a certain age to reach top levels of performance, especially sports.

Practice also seems most important in fields that are predictable and established. If you go into a new area, where there are no existing experts, then you'll be able to reach the forefront much faster. This is a major benefit of focusing on neglected areas. Likewise, practice is much more important for something predictable, like running, than for areas involving lots of novel situations, like responding to aviation crises.

Finally, in some areas, recognized experts don't actually obviously perform better than lay people, such as people who try to predict business events.[71] In these areas, success is due to other factors.

To find out more about how to make creative contributions to a field, we recommend *Originals* by Professor Adam Grant.

Conclusion

There's a huge amount anyone can do to make themselves more productive, happier and able to have a greater positive impact on the world. Do the steps above and you'll achieve more.

---

[71] For instance, see Tetlock's surveys of "expert" political and economic forecasters in "Expert Political Judgment: How Good Is It? How Can We Know?" which shows their predictions are rarely more accurate than chance.

APPENDIX 3

Four biases to avoid in career decisions

Over the last couple of decades, a large and growing body of research has emerged which shows that our decisions are far from rational.[72] We did a survey of this research to find out what it means for your career decisions.

It turns out that we likely don't know as much as we think we do, are overconfident, tend to think too narrowly and continue with paths that are no longer best for us. We need to be more skeptical of our decisions than we might be inclined to be, find ways to broaden our options, and take a more systematic and evidence-based approach to career choice.

In what follows, we summarize the main sources of bias and outline what you can do about them.

---

[72] For reviews of the literature, see Kahneman, D and Tversky, A (1974) "Judgement under Uncertainty: Heuristics and Biases", Science, New Series, Vol. 185, No. 4157, pp. 1124-1131, and the books "Thinking Fast and Slow" by Daniel Kahneman and "Predictably Irrational" by Dan Ariely.

1. Thinking narrowly

We often think too narrowly when considering what options are available to us, and what's important in comparing them.

What's the evidence for this?

There's evidence that in decision-making, we "narrow frame" in two ways: first, we think too narrowly about what options are available to us. Second, we think too narrowly about what our objectives are in comparing those options.[73] This is supported both by direct studies, and by the existence of more general biases: the availability heuristic, causing us to focus on options that are readily available; anchoring, a tendency to overweight the first piece of information given; status quo bias, an irrational preference for the current state of affairs; and the sunk cost fallacy, the tendency to assign more weight to options we've already invested time and effort into.

Why is it a problem for careers?

If people consistently fail to think through all the opportunities available to them, it seems likely that many people could be in better-suited and higher impact careers than they are currently.

As explained above, it's not just about missing options: it's about how you compare them. If you neglect an important

---

[73] See Richard P. Larrick, "Broaden the decision frame to make effective decisions" in "Handbook of Principles of Organizational Behaviour: Indispensable Knowledge for Evidence-Based Management" (2009) edited by Edwin A. Locke, Second Edition, Wiley.

consideration when comparing options, you might end up favoring the wrong one for the wrong reasons. There's risk of a compound effect here: first thinking too narrowly about what options are available to you and then on top of this, thinking too narrowly about how to evaluate this already limited set of options – your chances of choosing a suboptimal career are greatly increased.

What can you do about it?

Take some time to broaden your horizons. Use frameworks to brainstorm new options, such as those suggested on our 'how to choose' page (http://80k.link/HWC). Widen your perspective by talking to and comparing options with other people: the more diverse the range of people you consult, the better. As well as thinking through the pros of each of your options, think too about why they might not be so great: what are some reasons you might be wrong about this option?

2. Getting stuck

We often continue on paths or in careers for too long when it would actually be more beneficial to change.

What's the evidence for this?

A bias known as the sunk cost fallacy: a tendency to continue doing something that's no longer beneficial simply because we've already invested a lot of time or money in it.[74]

---

[74] See Arkes, H and Blumer, C, "The Psychology of Sunk Cost", (1985) Organizational Behaviour and Human Decision Processes 35, pp. 124-140.

This is irrational because the time or money is already spent, and therefore irrelevant to the decision you're now making: they are sunk costs.

Why is it a problem for careers?

Suppose you've spent years working and studying to get a dream job, only to realize you could be doing something completely different that would have much more impact. The thought of abandoning all those years' effort is hard, right? It's tempting to continue with what you've already invested in, hoping things will improve. But you can't get the years you've spent already back: and by continuing you're probably just wasting more. Abandoning sunk costs in your career can be incredibly difficult, but it's important if you want to make as much difference as possible. You need to be able to identify when your preference for a certain career is for good reason, and when it's just because of past commitments.

What can you do about it?

The bad news is that it doesn't seem like simply knowing about the sunk cost fallacy, thinking hard about it, or talking it over with people, will help very much. The good news, though, is that sunk costs can be fought if you try hard enough and think about your decisions in the right way:

- **Ignore the past:** think about where you are now, the qualifications and experience you have, as if they just appeared from nowhere.
- **Think about the future:** make a list of the pros and cons of each of your alternatives *from now on.*
- **Justify your decision to someone else:** it's much harder to justify biased decisions to someone else!

3. Misjudging your chances

We're likely to misjudge our chances of success in different career paths.

What's the evidence for this?

When judging our chances of success, we tend to use something called the representativeness heuristic: asking "how much do I *seem* like the sort of person who would be successful in this field?" The problem with this approach is that, no matter how much you look like the kind of person who would be successful, if the chances of *anyone* succeeding in your field are low, you'll likely be overestimating your chances. This is known as base rate neglect: neglecting to consider the underlying probabilities or base rates. No matter how much you *seem* like the sort of person who would single-handedly find a cure for cancer, your chances of doing so are small simply because the chances of *anyone* doing so are so small.

There's also evidence from studies that we tend to be overconfident in general: most people think they're better than average, and underestimate the time it will take them to complete a given task.

Why is it a problem for careers?

Being successful in whatever you do is obviously crucial to making an impact. The existence of base rate neglect plus overconfidence suggest that we're likely to overestimate our chances of finding a cure for malaria, becoming head of the world's most cost-effective charity, or completely revolutionizing academic incentives, to give a few examples.

But this doesn't mean that no-one should do these things.[75] What we need is to be able to accurately judge our chances of success: aiming high, but not too high.

What can you do about it?

The suggested approach should help you judge your chances of success in a given field or career:[76]

1. Work out which factors (personality traits, skills and abilities) are most relevant to success in the field you're considering.
2. Find ways to objectively measure yourself on these factors.
3. Given this information, narrow down your reference class to those similar to you.
4. Get your "base rate" from this class.

4. Relying too much on your gut

Although conventional wisdom emphasizes the importance of "going with your gut" in career decisions, we should be skeptical of at least some of our intuitive judgements.

---

[75] Plus there's evidence that overconfidence, and optimism bias in general, can have its benefits: being overconfident might actually increase our chances of success by causing us to take risks and work harder. How much optimism is optimal? We're unsure, but it's likely to be better to be overconfident rather than underconfident.

[76] For more detail on how to do this, see 80000hours.org/2012/12/how-to-judge-your-chances-of-success.

What can you do about it?

Double-check your intuitions against more systematic methods and get more evidence. You might, for example, try explicitly listing all the factors that are important for your decision, and then attempt to score different options on these factors and compare them. Even if you don't necessarily use this to determine your decision, it will likely highlight some factors that your first impressions miss, and flag the areas where you need to get more information.

APPENDIX 4

Our decision framework

In order to find a fulfilling career that makes a difference to the world, what should you be looking for in your options? We'll set out how to compare options using our four-part career framework.

How can we compare different careers?

Short-term impact

Let's start by considering your impact only in the short-term. We can break it into two components:

1. Role-impact – the extent to which the role gives you opportunities to have a large social impact.
2. Personal fit – the extent to which *you* will be able to take advantage of these opportunities.

We think these two factors roughly multiply, i.e. if you're twice as good at the role, then your overall impact will be twice as high.

Long-term impact

However, we also care about your long-run potential to make an impact. This also breaks down into two factors:

1. Career capital – the extent to which the role gives you opportunities to put yourself in a better position to make an impact in the future.
2. Personal fit – the extent to which you will be able to take advantage of these opportunities.

Personal satisfaction

So far we've only discussed social impact, but what about your personal satisfaction? We know that job satisfaction is important for your long-run social impact, because if you don't enjoy your job you're more likely to burn out.

As we discuss in Chapter 1, if you find work that you're good at and that helps others, then you'll already be a long way towards a fulfilling career. Gaining career capital is also important for your personal success and growth.

However, there are some extra ingredients of job satisfaction that aren't fully covered by the factors already listed. These include having engaging work that absorbs your attention, working with people you like, the job meeting your basic needs (with regards to salary, working hours, etc.) and it fitting with the rest of your life. To cover these, we include "supportive conditions" as a separate factor, and include all of these matters under it.

If we factor the role-impact and personal fit components out of job satisfaction, then we can write the whole set of factors as follows:

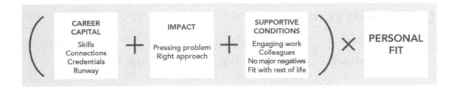

How can we weigh these factors?

Here are some tips for balancing the different factors against each other:

- If you are still early in your career, then it's best to place greater importance on career capital than on role-impact, as you're likely to be able to find plenty of good opportunities to invest in yourself. If you're late in your career, place less importance on career capital and more on making an impact now. That said, the amount of weight to put on career capital also depends on the urgency of the problems you want to focus on.

- The more uncertain you are about the long run, the more you should prioritize flexible career capital over narrow career capital. Flexible career capital is career capital that's useful in many different roles.

- The more altruistically-minded you are, the less weight you'll need to place on the supportive conditions relative to the other factors.

- Bear in mind that personal fit is potentially the most important factor because it can improve everything else.

The value of exploration

Career decisions are highly uncertain, and so often the most valuable thing you can do is learn more about your options.

That way, you'll be able to make better decisions in the long run.

Sometimes this means that it can be worth taking an option just as an experiment. For this reason, in the past, we sometimes added "exploration value" to the framework. Today, we think this is a little confusing, so we took it out (instead, we factored it into our advice in Chapter 6). However, we still think the idea is right – often the most important thing is to try out lots of options.

How to use the framework

When it comes to figuring out which job is best for you, we're heavily in favor of investigating and experimenting with different options, rather than trying to figure it all out ahead of time. However, you're likely to have limited time to investigate, so you'll need some way to do an initial elimination of options.

In addition, if your investigations are not conclusive, then ultimately you'll need to make an in-depth assessment of each option on your shortlist.

You'll want to start by doing an initial ranking using your intuition.

Then, assess your options based on:

- Personal fit
- Role-impact
- Career capital
- Job satisfaction
- Other personal factors not included in the above.

If you're just doing an initial cut-down, eliminate anything that does really badly on one of the factors, or is dominated by an alternative (i.e. does worse or equal on all the factors).

If you're doing a more detailed assessment, it's usually helpful to score your options from one to five on each of these factors. You might find that this reveals a clear winner. If not, it can still help you to think more deeply about your options and get feedback from others – show them your scores and ask them if you've made a mistake.

Bear in mind that you'll want to focus your assessment on the factors that are most decisive for your particular decision. This might mean cutting down the list and making it more specific.

You can also add all your scores together and rank your options based on that. There are reasons to think that this will be more accurate than just going with your intuition to decide which option is best. That said, don't just blindly go with the total score. If your intuition is telling you that the result is wrong, try to figure out why. In some situations, your gut instinct can be more accurate than conscious reasoning (e.g. when it comes to social situations) while in others analytical thinking is more accurate.

To improve accuracy, look at each score in turn and ask yourself "why might this be wrong?" or try to justify it to a friend.

216

Questions for assessing each factor

Here are some questions to consider when assessing each factor.

Personal fit

Start by trying to work out the typical odds of a person succeeding in this area – the base rate. Then ask whether you're more or less likely to succeed than average:

- What are the best predictors of success in this field? Do any apply to you?
- Does this path make use of your most valuable career capital? Does it play to your special edge?
- If you totally failed for a year or two, could you easily imagine persisting?

Role-impact

We usually break this down into the following questions (impact potential is proportional to the multiple of the two):

1. How pressing is the problem? This can be further broken down into:
   a. Is it big in scale?
   b. Is it neglected by others?
   c. How possible is it to make progress?
2. How large a contribution can you make to the problem? This can be further broken down into:
   a. Contribution through your direct work
   b. Contribution through your donations
   c. Contribution through using your position for advocacy

Some other rules of thumb to consider are:

- Will you have flexibility over which problems you work on?
- Have people who've had a lot of impact pursued this route in the past?
- Do people neglect this path for bad reasons?

See Chapter 4 for a list of the four types of influential career.

Career capital

This can be broken down into:

1. **Skills** – what will you learn in this job? You can break skills down into transferable skills, knowledge and personality traits. You'll learn fastest in jobs where you receive good mentorship.

2. **Connections** – who will you work with and meet in this job? It's important to make connections who are both influential and who care about social impact.

3. **Credentials** – will this job act as a good signal to future collaborators or employers? Note that we don't just mean formal credentials like having a law degree, but also your achievements and reputation. If you're a writer, it's the quality of your blog. If you're a coder, it's your GitHub.

4. **Runway** – how much money will you save in this job? Your runway is how long you could comfortably live with no income. We recommend aiming for at least six months of runway to maintain your financial security.

12-18 months of runway is even more useful because it gives you the flexibility to make a major career change.

And don't forget to consider:

- How good will this career capital be for taking you towards your medium-term goals?
- How flexible is the career capital? Will it be useful in many future jobs?

See Chapter 5 for a list of good options for career capital.

Supportive conditions

This can be broken down into:

- (Impact and personal fit – already covered above)
- Engaging work – will you get freedom to decide how to work, clear tasks, clear feedback and variety in what you do?
- Colleagues – will you like them and will they support you?
- Basic needs – will you earn enough money, will the hours be reasonable, will the commute be reasonable?
- Fit with rest of life – will you be able to improve your personal relationships, and uphold any other important personal priorities?

Read more about job satisfaction in Chapter 1.

APPENDIX 5

How to do high-impact research

If you have good personal fit for a pressing area of research, it can be one of the highest-impact career options. Here we explore how best to do it.

What research should you do early career?

Lots of people want to do high impact research while still a graduate student or postdoc. That's great if it's possible, but it's even more important to first establish your career. When we interviewed top biomedical researchers, this was a major theme of their advice.

In the current academic system, it's very important to develop a strong publications record early, so do what you can to make that happen. It's also important to get great training, so seek out a top research group who will mentor you, even if it's not the area you'd ideally work long-term.

What are the highest impact research topics?

As your career becomes more established, you'll gain more and more freedom to choose the topics you want to work on. Which should you choose?

Personal fit is especially important in research, because the most productive researchers have far more output than the median (as we argue below). Aim for a field where you have a realistic chance of being in the top 10%, and ideally top 1%. It could be worth entering a "low-impact" area if you have good enough personal fit.

However, all else equal, it's best to enter an area that's also pressing i.e. where there are problems to work on that are big in scale, neglected and where you can see an avenue towards progress.

Looking at the intersection of two fields is another method that seems to have a track record of success. You can also look at areas where new techniques are making new research possible.

Among the areas we've reviewed so far, we'd pick the following (roughly in order, starting with the highest impact):

- Risks from artificial intelligence
- Global priorities research
- Developing meat substitutes
- Biosecurity
- Understanding and preventing tail risks from climate change
- Development economics
- Biomedical research

Some others we expect are promising but which we haven't reviewed yet include:

- Improving scientific practice
- Improving collective decision making
- Cheap green energy
- Democratic reform
- Developing policy to increase international migration

This list is nowhere near exclusive. We expect that there are high impact topics in most fields. Often only experts in a field can spot which topics are high-impact.

Should you become a researcher?

Research seems to be an area where the most successful people have far more impact than the rest:

1. Some researchers publish scientific papers at a rate at least fifty times greater than others, and the distribution appears to be log normal.

2. This is what we would expect if publishing papers was a multiplicative function of several independent skills, which seems reasonable.

3. The distribution of citations is very peaked: the top 0.1% of papers have 1000 citations, compared to about 1 citation per paper at the median. This distribution may be more skewed than the true distribution of impact per paper, because it's exaggerated by feedback effects in which one paper becomes the standard paper that everyone cites. Nevertheless, we expect it's still the case

that some papers are vastly more influential than others.

4. Senior researchers generally believe large differences in output exist. Some who we interviewed said that a "good researcher" was rare and valuable. Prof. Townsend used the phrase "worth their weight in gold." Prof. Todd said "One good guy can cover the ground of 5, and I'm not exaggerating." And these people were talking about researchers who are already in a top lab.

This means the key determinant of whether you should enter research is personal fit. If you have some chance of being a top researcher, then it's likely among the highest impact paths. If not, then you could probably do more by earning to give and funding research, or something else.

If you're unsure, then continue with academia. Generally it's hard to re-enter the academic path once you've left it, especially after a PhD (though it varies a bit by field e.g. computer scientists sometimes switch back and forth between academia and industry; economists switch back and forth between academia and policy). This means that if you're truly in doubt about whether to stay in academia, it's best to lean towards staying to preserve flexibility.

We say "truly in doubt" because continuing in academia is usually seen as the default, high-status path – at least when you're still in academia – so probably more people do it than they should.

How can you work out your degree of personal fit?

The best indicator is you track record. Test yourself step-by-step:

1. At undergraduate level, you should aim for top grades (a 1st in the UK, or GPA over 3.5 in the US).
2. Try to do a research project one summer and see whether you like it.
3. At graduate level, what was your class rank?
4. Ideally, at the end of your PhD, you're the author of an article in a top journal and have a strong reference from your supervisor.

Some other predictors that seem important:

- Particularly high intelligence.
- High levels of grit and self-motivation, to persist for years in the face of a high chance of failure.
- Deep intrinsic interest in the relevant subject matter.

Don't forget non-academic positions

There are many research positions outside of academia, which can be more fulfilling because your work has more tangible impact and will involve more teamwork.

Some paths to consider include:

- If you want to transfer into business but still do research, data science is a path we've seen work well.

- There are many positions in companies that develop important technology e.g. Gilead Sciences developed drugs to treat HIV and Hepatitis; Tesla is developing cheaper batteries.

- Think tanks if you want to enter policy e.g. the Center for Global Development has had a significant influence on development policy.

- International organizations e.g. the World Bank.

- Non-traditional academia – work in academia funded by 2-4 year grants, rather than by taking a traditional academic position that comes with a teaching load (e.g. the Future of Humanity Institute in Oxford).

APPENDIX 6

Should you wait to make a difference?

If you're committed to making a difference with your career, you may well find that there is a tension between doing good now and laying the groundwork for doing good later.

For example:

- Next year, you have two choices. You could work for an effective charity, making an immediate difference to its beneficiaries. Or you could go to graduate school and build up your career capital, (hopefully) allowing you to have a larger impact later.

- Alternatively, say you have a substantial sum of money. You could give it today, or you could invest it, allow it to grow, and then give the larger amount later.

How can you go about deciding between these options? Here we present a summary of our findings. The full research has been published by Oxford University's Global Priorities Project (globalprioritiesproject.org/2015/02/give-now-or-later).

Summary: should you donate money now or later?

First, focus on saving enough to live for at least 6 months with no income, then start making a reasonable level of retirement savings (typical advice is 15% of income) and paying down any high interest rate debt. During this period, aim to give 1% so you stay engaged with giving and keep learning about which charities are most effective.

After that, whether to give now or later depends on a couple of factors. If you're very uncertain about where's most effective to give, then it's probably best to invest the money and give it later. We'd recommend doing this in a donor-advised fund to save tax (there's a guide at www.benkuhn.net /giving-101#donor-advised-funds).

If you've decided on a problem area, then it depends on how urgent the problem is. If it's a rapidly growing, unexplored area, then it's probably important to donate sooner rather than later. If it's a more established area, then it's probably better to compound your money and donate later.

This is especially true early in your career, because there are probably ways you can invest in yourself that could have a big return, such as: graduate study, doing a programming bootcamp, or spending money to meet people who can boost your career e.g. by going to the right conferences.

Summary: Should you give your time now or later?

Early career, we recommend focusing on building career capital because we think there's generally a lot you can do to improve your skills and put yourself in a much better position to make a difference long-term.

During this period, however, try to stay engaged with other people who want to do good, so you keep learning about social impact and stick to your values. (And ideally find something that both builds career capital and has a social impact.)

After that, the balance again depends on which problems you think are most pressing. If the problems are more urgent, then focus more on short-run impact, and otherwise focus on career capital.

If you're very uncertain about which problems are most pressing, then focus on building flexible career capital e.g. learn transferable skills like marketing and management.

The main factors in more depth

Diminishing opportunities for good

The main argument for doing good now is that the best opportunities are getting snapped up, so that the longer you wait, the harder it will be to have the same impact with your work or your donation. Opportunities for bigger and easier interventions are likely to be taken sooner, before it's considered worthwhile to look into smaller and more difficult areas.

Increased understanding of interventions

On the other hand, research continually improves our understanding of which interventions are likely to be effective. As a result, the opportunities for doing good may actually increase over time: just because an intervention is big and easy, doesn't mean anyone even knew it was possible 20 years ago!

Returns on investment

Another critical factor to consider is the extent to which investing your time or your money will give increased returns in the future. Invested money will increase at a pretty standard rate throughout your life. By contrast, the rewards for investing in yourself are likely to be much higher if you prioritize this early in your career: many people dramatically increase their ability to earn and change the world in their first twenty years of work by learning skills, gaining promotions, studying further and building networks.

If there are plenty of good opportunities to invest in yourself, as is often the case early on in your career, then our recommendation is that it makes sense to wait. You'll have more impact in the long-term by prioritizing your career capital now, then focusing on making a difference later. (Although we don't advocate neglecting doing good entirely: see the section on burning out below.)

Certainty about the effectiveness of causes

How certain are you are in your views about which causes are the best? If your views are unstable, this tends to point towards waiting until you are more certain. Otherwise, you could give up opportunities for investment, only to find out that the cause you've been supporting isn't that effective after all!

The exception to this is if giving will allow you to learn more. This might involve working in or funding causes you think are contenders to be the best, or funding comparisons between them. This option is particularly good if you can get information that will help not just you but other people in similar situations. In this case we think that the best option is likely to be to give now to improve your knowledge about which causes are best.

The attention causes have received

Just as opportunities to do good diminish in general (as set out earlier), they will also diminish within a particular cause. The result is that the more attention a cause has already received (in terms of research, man hours, donations etc.), the less effective additional resources will be.

Therefore in areas where little has been done, and which therefore have the potential for fast growth, helping now may be particularly valuable: if you wait, the best work may already have been done. By contrast, in areas which are well-established, the difference between helping now and helping later is likely to be less pronounced.

One area where this recommendation is ambiguous is in cost-effectiveness focused global poverty interventions. Development aid as a whole is a large area which is not quickly growing, but it may be that the proportion of spending which is directed towards the most cost-effective interventions is increasing quickly. It's unclear which is the more appropriate reference class, and we are not confident whether it's better to give now or later in this case.

Other considerations

The factors considered above are the main ones, but they are not exhaustive. Below are a couple of other points worth considering.

Not burning out

Even if you are focusing on giving later, it may well be best to do something now in order to avoid burning out or getting out of the habit of doing good. Doing good can make you happier, help you to stay motivated, and bring others on board by demonstrating your commitment.

So, it seems advisable to stay involved in making a difference in at least some capacity, perhaps by donating 10% of your income, befriending other altruistic people, and making a public declaration of your intention to lead a high-impact career. In a similar way if you are giving now it may still be worth holding on to some investment as personal reserves.

Tax considerations

You can only claim tax relief against this year's income, which means you'll get more tax relief if you give now. However, you can get around this issue by putting your funds into a Donor Advised Fund. There could also be other tax considerations that push one way or the other.

APPENDIX 7

Advice for undergraduates (and potential undergraduates)

Here are some preliminary findings about how to choose an undergraduate course, and what to do once you start studying. It's based on our general knowledge and the experiences of people we've advised. We haven't yet done in-depth research into this area, so our views could easily change.

Priorities

As an undergraduate, you're right at the start of your career, so it makes sense to focus mainly on exploring promising future career options and building flexible career capital, rather than pursuing any specific option. This is especially true because your undergraduate years are a great time to explore - you have a lot of flexibility over your time, your minor courses, long summer holidays, and the possibility of a year abroad or gap year.

Look to learn things that will be useful in almost any future career path. Write a list of five areas you'd like to explore during undergraduate, then figure out how you can try them all out. Also consider trying one or two wildcard options –

unusual paths outside your main areas of experience that might help you spot new considerations (see Chapter 6 for more tips about exploring).

Which degree subject?

Weigh up your options primarily in terms of:

1. **Personal fit** – will you be good at the subject? If you're good at the subject, it's more likely you'll be able to pursue work in that area later on, you'll enjoy it more, you'll get better grades, and you'll do the work more quickly.
2. **Flexibility of the program** – does it open up lots of options, both inside and outside academia?

If you're unsure about personal fit, try out the subject (e.g. through an online course, or in a minor course).

So which subjects offer the most options and flexibility?

- One indicator is earnings prospects. In general, more applied, quantitative subjects have the highest earnings, even if you adjust for the intelligence of the people studying different subjects.[77]

- However, some subjects gain earnings at the expense of flexibility. Petroleum engineers have among the highest earnings, but their fate is tied to a single (declining?) industry. In general, more "fundamental" subjects

---

[77] Read more at econlog.econlib.org/archives/2013/04/major_premium.html.

provide more flexibility. For instance, you can go from economics into the rest of the social sciences, but the reverse is harder. People with applied math skills probably have the most flexibility - they can go into areas like biology, physics, economics, computer science and psychology. The worst options for flexibility are narrow applied options, such as nursing or education.

- Some subjects are more prestigious than others, especially those perceived as "difficult", like math, medicine and philosophy.

Some other, less important, factors to consider include:

- Relevance of the option to your longer term plans e.g. if you want to become a medic, you'll need to study pre-med. Flexibility is more important than relevance, but it's also worth considering.

- Difficulty of learning this subject outside of university - some subjects are hard to study by yourself, either because they require lots of feedback, discipline, or cumulative background knowledge. This is most pronounced with quantitative technical skills, like statistics, and mathematical modeling. It also applies to skills like understanding the law and accounting, and being good at writing.

Putting all this together:

- We think it's reasonable to aim for the most fundamental, quantitative option you can do i.e. one of these in the following order: mathematics, economics, computer science, physics, engineering, political science / chemistry / biology.

- If you want to focus on something non-quantitative, then consider focusing on developing great written communication skills in philosophy, history or English.

- If you want to do something more applied, then maybe business or accounting.

- A good combination seems to be a major in a quantitative subject and a minor in a subject that requires great written skills (e.g. major in math and minor in philosophy). We say this because people who can both understand quantitative topics and communicate clearly seem highly in-demand in all kinds of areas.

How much time to spend studying?

If you want to keep the option of academia open, and keep open some professional courses like law and medicine, then you need top grades (1st class honors in the UK, or GPA over 3.6 in the US).

However, many employers (e.g. many professional services positions) are satisfied with middling grades (2.1 in the UK, or GPA over 3.0 in the US). Or you might want to be self-employed. In these case, it's probably more important to do internships and impressive extracurricular activities.

What to do outside your degree?

1. Explore options you're interested in longer term – learn about other subjects, do internships and summer jobs, volunteer, travel. (And also consider exploring some "wildcard" options you know little about).

2. Build lasting friendships – university is perhaps your single best opportunity to make lifelong friends, and they're extremely important for your long-term happiness and success. Once you start work, you have far less time to hang out with new people, and you won't meet as many people similar to you. We know lots of people who regret not spending more time meeting people while at university.

3. Invest in your career capital – especially in ways that will be useful no matter what career you end up in. See Chapter 5 for more detail.

4. Extracurricular options that build skills and look good - run a student society; start a microbusiness; or do anything you'll be good at and get impressive achievements within.

Should you go to college at all?

On average, in financial terms, college is a great investment. Researchers on this topic widely agree that going to college significantly boosts your income, even after you account for (i) lost earnings while studying (ii) the fact that the people who go to college are often more able, which means they'll earn more anyway.[78]

Our guess is that this boost reflects a general increase in your career capital – not only will you earn more, you'll also be more productive and influential. Moreover, the boost seems large enough that it's (i) likely better than what else you could be doing to boost your career capital (ii) likely better to make the investment rather than try to make a difference sooner.

We don't know what causes the boost. It's likely a combination of the skills you learn, the fact that employers value the credential, or the connections you make, but we're not sure which is most important.

What are the exceptions?

1. College doesn't offer great returns if you're likely to drop out. If you'd struggle with the academic demands, or really not enjoy it, then consider not going. If you think you wouldn't enjoy college, bear in mind there are lots of different types of college and social scene, which can provide very different experiences.[79]

2. You've found a more effective way to build your career capital. These opportunities seem very rare, but they do exist. For instance, we've met people who learned to program and skipped college. This can work because the technology industry doesn't care so much about formal credentials (though you're still betting your career on one industry). Getting a Thiel Fellowship is another example.

---

[78] For more information see 80000hours.org/2014/01/the-value-of-a-degree.

[79] Read more at econlog.econlib.org/archives/2014/09/what_every_high.html.

3. You've found an urgent opportunity to do good. In that case, it might be better to delay going to college to do good right away. For instance, you have a startup project that's taking off.

In most cases, if you think you've found something better than going to college, it's best to start college, do the project on the side, then leave if it takes off. This is what famous drop-outs like Bill Gates did.

Which type of university should you go to?

One famous study in the US found that students who were accepted to an "elite" university but turned it down, went on to earn just as much. This suggests that elite universities are selecting more talented people, but not actually helping them be more successful (with the exception of low-income students, who did earn more).

It could be that the benefits of elite universities are mainly offset by other costs, such as an increased chance of burning out. Or perhaps talented students at non-elite universities get more attention from professors. Given that elite universities also cost more, the choice is not obvious.

On the other hand, it could be that the main benefits of elite universities are not reflected in income.

We find it hard to believe that elite universities don't offer significant benefits. Attending an elite university is widely seen as a good credential by employers. Most importantly, there are more opportunities to meet other talented students at elite universities, helping you build much better connections.

Overall, we think it's still better to try to attend an elite university, but we're not sure.

You can get more information on how to compare different institutions using "value-added" rankings, such as the one provided by the Economist for the U.S.[80]

There's also evidence that an elite university degree is helpful if you do a liberal arts major or business degree but not if you major in science.[81] This could be because arts subjects are harder to evaluate, so employers resort to credentials to compare candidates. Your network might also be more important outside of science. So, if you want to study science, going to a good value state college is a decent option.

Finally, bear in mind that your choice of major is similarly important to your choice of university, so it could be better to do your preferred major at a less prestigious university.

---

[80] www.economist.com/blogs/graphicdetail/2015/10/value-university

[81] See wsj.com/articles/do-elite-colleges-lead-to-higher-salaries-only-for-some-professions-1454295674.

APPENDIX 8

Career review summaries

As part of our research, we've evaluated different careers: how likely people are to succeed in them, how much good they could do in them, and how to enter them.

The following summaries reflect our full career reviews as of August 2016, which can be found on our website. If any of them sound interesting, we strongly recommend that you go online to view the full and most up-to-date reviews at:

http://80k.link/J3T

Actuarial science

Actuarial science could be a good option for someone who wants to earn to give, has strong quantitative skills, and values security and work-life balance.

However, someone capable of pursuing an actuarial career should also consider quantitative finance, which offers higher expected earnings, spending a few years in management consulting, which offers superior flexibility and prestige, or training for data science, which offers more flexibility and opportunity for direct impact.

Pros:

- Reasonably high salary and reliable employment.
- Moderate intensity of work allows for a long-lasting career and even side-projects.
- High chances of career progression.

Cons:

- Little opportunity for direct impact or advocacy, though we doubt actuarial careers are harmful.
- Lower prestige and salary growth than some adjacent careers requiring similar skills.
- Professional certification exams require impressive quantitative skills.

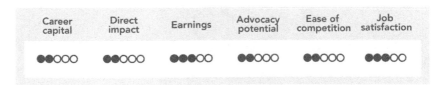

Career capital	Direct impact	Earnings	Advocacy potential	Ease of competition	Job satisfaction
●●○○○	●●○○○	●●●○○	●●○○○	●●○○○	●●●○○

Key facts on fit

Strong quantitative and computer skills, attention to detail, willing to have social impact mostly through donations.

Next steps

Admission to a Master's course or trainee position will usually require having done well in a significant number of quantitative courses, such as mathematics, economics or finance as an undergraduate.

Professional bodies in all major countries offer guides to becoming actuaries, and you should read them for details.

Full profile

80000hours.org/career-reviews/actuarial-science

Biomedical research

Biomedical researchers investigate how the human body works with the aim of finding new ways to improve health. Biomedical research has likely produced large returns to society per researcher in the past. We expect it to continue to be a high impact area in the future, and it appears to be constrained by good researchers. Its drawbacks are that it takes a long time to train, has high drop-out rates and leaves you relatively fixed in the biomedical field. You should strongly consider this path if you have an undergraduate degree from a top university with high grades (GPA 3.8+), you've tested your fit for research by doing a placement in a lab, and you have a place on a top-ten PhD program for your specialty. However, success in this path is very hard to predict, so we encourage you to have a backup plan.

Pros:

- Biomedical research is a promising cause area.
- The field seems to be constrained by good researchers.
- Highly interesting work for the intellectually curious.

Cons:

- Long time to train (four to twelve years).
- Highly competitive – people drop out even in their late thirties and forties.
- Relatively narrow exit options.

Career capital	Direct impact	Earnings	Advocacy potential	Ease of competition	Job satisfaction
●●○○○	●●●●○	●●●○○	●●●○○	●○○○○	●●●○○

Key facts on fit

Very high intelligence, intense intellectual curiosity and interest in biomedical research, grit, programming and statistics in demand.

Next steps

Contact lab managers during your 2nd or 3rd year at university to get a job as a research assistant in a lab to test your fit. Then apply to PhD programs.

Full profile

80000hours.org/career-reviews/biomedical-research

Computer Science PhD

A computer science PhD offers the chance to become a leading researcher in a highly important field with potential for transformational research. Especially consider it if you want to enter computer science academia or do high-level research in industry and expect to be among the top 30% of PhD candidates.

Pros:

- Potential for large impact from your research.
- Opportunity to become an expert in AI.
- Freedom to pursue research topics that most interest you.
- Very smart colleagues.
- Helps you enter technical jobs in industry, providing a backup to academia (though if industry is your aim, it's probably better to enter directly).

Cons:

- Less than 10% end up with tenure-track jobs.
- Takes a long time (five to seven years), with relatively low pay.
- Doing highly open-ended research provides little feedback which can be demotivating.
- About half of those who enter industry afterwards don't end up with research positions.

Career capital	Direct impact	Earnings	Advocacy potential	Ease of competition	Job satisfaction
●●●○○	●●●○○	●○○○○	●●●○○	●○○○○	●●●○○

Key facts on fit

Strong quantitative skills (i.e. above 650 on quantitative GRE), want to enter high-level computer science research roles, extremely interested in computer science research.

Next steps

If you are interested, try out doing computer science research by doing a dissertation as an undergraduate or taking up research assistant jobs in a professor's lab.

Full profile

80000hours.org/career-reviews/computer-science-phd

Data science (for skill-building & earning to give)

If you have a PhD in a quantitative subject (or if you're the type of person who would enjoy a quantitative PhD), but are not sure you want to go into academia, consider data science. It can provide the intellectual satisfaction of research, but with more immediate, tangible results, and more team work. And you'll get a great skill-set that's increasingly in demand in a wide variety of important areas.

Pros:

- Gain the ability to generate actionable insights from the increasing amount of data collected by humanity, opening the opportunity to contribute to progress across a wide range of causes.
- Develop undersupplied skills in programming, machine learning and statistics, for which demand is forecast to grow rapidly, opening many options.
- Cultures of learning and mentorship, often reasonable and flexible hours.
- High starting salaries – graduates of data science bootcamp Zipfian Academy earn $115K on average.

Cons:

- A large portion of time is spent on cleaning data, which most find unexciting.

- Pressure to find and deliver immediately actionable insights, less scope for longer-term exploratory research.

Career capital	Direct impact	Earnings	Advocacy potential	Ease of competition	Job satisfaction
●●●●○	●●●○○	●●●○○	●●○○○	●●○○○	●●●○○

Key facts on fit

Strong quantitative skills (e.g. would consider doing a science PhD), strong interest in applied research, able to communicate technical ideas clearly to non-technical audiences.

Next steps

You can easily test your fit for this career by taking an introduction to data science course. You can enter either by self-learning, building a portfolio of projects on a blog and GitHub and applying to companies directly, or you can take a data science bootcamp. In the US, the two best known bootcamps for PhD holders are Insight Data Science (insightdatascience.com) and The Data Incubator (thedataincubator.com), and for those without a PhD, Zipfian Academy (zipfianacademy.com). Signal Data Science (signaldatascience.com) is a new bootcamp run by supporters of 80,000 Hours. In the UK there is ASI Fellowship (theasi.co/fellowship) (also run by supporters of 80,000 Hours) and Science to Data Science (s2ds.org), both of which usually only accept PhD holders.

Full profile

80000hours.org/career-reviews/data-science

Economics PhD

An economics PhD is one of the most attractive graduate programs: if you get through, you have a high chance of landing a good research job in academia or policy – promising areas for social impact – and you have backup options in the corporate sector since the skills you learn are in demand (unlike many PhD programs). You should especially consider an economics PhD if you want to go into research roles, are good at math (i.e. quantitative GRE score above 165) and have a proven interest in economics research.

Pros:

- Decent chance of entering economics academia, which has potential for highly valuable research and the option of working on topics in related social sciences.
- In demand by think tanks, government departments and international organizations (e.g. IMF, World Bank).
- Gain a broad set of tools for understanding how the social world works and evaluating causes and interventions.
- High degree of autonomy when writing your dissertation.
- Backup options in the corporate sector.

Cons:

- Takes a long time (five to seven years), with low pay.
- Doing highly open-ended research provides little feedback which can be demotivating.

Career capital	Direct impact	Earnings	Advocacy potential	Ease of competition	Job satisfaction
●●●●○	●●●○○	●○○○○	●●●○○	●●○○○	●●●○○

Key facts on fit

Strong math skills (i.e. 165+ on quantitative GRE), want to enter high-level research roles, prepared to work long hours.

Next steps

You can test your ability and interest by taking classes in economics, math and statistics either at your university or online. You don't need an economics undergraduate degree to enter but proven math ability is required, so make sure you study quantitative subjects.

Full profile

80000hours.org/career-reviews/economics-phd

Executive search

Executive Search firms aim to fill senior roles within other organizations, most often large companies or professional services firms.

We think executive search (AKA headhunting) could be a good option for those who want to earn to give, desire work-life balance, and whose main strengths are verbal and social skills.

Nonetheless, we don't recommend executive search to many people because the career capital and exit options are weaker than nearby alternatives.

Pros:

- High pay relative to how competitive it is, making it a promising option for earning to give, especially if you're not good with numbers.
- Reasonable working hours.
- Opportunity to build a strong personal network.

Cons:

- The skills developed are more narrow, and the field is less prestigious than other professional services. As a result, exit opportunities are weaker than alternatives like consulting or marketing.
- The social impact is likely to be small unless you recruit for firms that are themselves high impact.

Career capital	Direct impact	Earnings	Advocacy potential	Ease of competition	Job satisfaction
●●○○○	●●○○○	●●●○○	●●●○○	●●●●○	●●●●○

Key facts on fit

Social and verbal skills, professionalism and similarity to clients, extroversion.

Next steps

There are two main routes into this career:

1. After completing a degree with almost any major, you can apply for researcher roles at the largest firms, such as Korn Ferry International, Spencer Stuart and Heidrick & Struggles. For technology firms, the leaders are The Up Group and Renovata Partners; for financial services, Blackwood is the largest; for legal firms, options include Piper Pritchard, Hedley May, Fox Rodney, Major Lindsey and Africa. UK-only firms include Sax Bam and MBS Group.

2. You can apply for associate or higher roles if you have previous recruitment, sales or marketing experience, or an MBA. You can also jump to a higher level later in your career, taking advantage of knowledge of an industry you have worked in. This is apparently a move some people make for better work-life balance.

Full profile

80000hours.org/career-reviews/executive-search

Foundation grant-maker

Foundation grant-makers help foundations decide where to make donations. They influence large amounts of money ($10M+/year at large foundations), though they are often highly constrained in where they can allocate grants. They can also influence the direction of non-profits, build expertise and connections in a cause and make use of generous donation-matching schemes for their personal giving. If you're able to get a position at a foundation working on a promising cause, especially at Program Officer level, it's a promising option.

Pros:

- Potential to improve allocation of grants made by foundations.
- Potential to influence direction of existing non-profits, and assist them by providing connections and basic oversight.
- Build expertise and a strong network in a cause, with potential to create new organizations, collaborations and projects.
- Decent salaries and donation-matching enable earning to give.
- Satisfying work with a socially motivated culture.

Cons:

- Usually constrained on cause where you can make grants, which reduces potential impact.
- Narrow experience in a single cause may be bad for keeping options open.
- Entry often requires advanced degrees and many years of narrow experience.

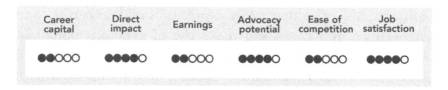

Career capital	Direct impact	Earnings	Advocacy potential	Ease of competition	Job satisfaction
●●○○○	●●●●○	●●○○○	●●●●○	●●○○○	●●●●○

Key facts on fit

Expertise in a cause area (3+ years' experience); well-rounded skill-profile, though interpersonal and communication skills especially important.

Next steps

You usually need experience in non-profits or think tanks that work in the cause area you want to join. You also often need a Master's in a relevant degree to your cause.

If you have the experience, ideally apply through referrals, using our standard advice.

Full profile

80000hours.org/career-reviews/foundation-program-manager

Founding effective non-profits (international development)

If you have gained expertise in a relevant area within international development, then we think there could be opportunities to found a non-profit that efficiently and transparently implements an evidence-backed intervention that doesn't already have a non-profit focused on it, and seeking funding from funders like GiveWell and Gates Foundation. This could lead to a large impact, while also giving you substantial opportunities to learn about development and build career capital.

Pros:

- Potential to have a large direct impact within international development.
- Builds expertise in international development, as well as generally valuable career capital.

Cons:

- It seems to take several years to build up the necessary expertise.
- The people who take this path seem highly able, suggesting it's very difficult.
- We're very uncertain how easy it is to find and take these opportunities before they would be exploited by other non-profits or governments.

Career capital	Direct impact	Earnings	Advocacy potential	Ease of competition	Job satisfaction
●●●●○	●●●●●	●●○○○	●●●○○	●○○○○	●●●●○

Key facts on fit

Well-rounded, risk-taking, very long hours, grit, independent, deep knowledge of relevant area.

Next steps

If you're at an early stage, focus on accumulating expertise and connections that put you in a better position to spot and take opportunities to found (e.g. a postgraduate degree, working on the ground, doing project management), while keeping your options open. Find out which interventions are developing an evidence-base but don't already have a non-profit focusing on them, and consider especially focusing your learning on these areas.

If you're considering founding, speak to GiveWell and Evidence Action, then the strategic development foundations such as Gates and CIFF. Aim to find out what conditions your organization would need to satisfy in order to get funding.

Full profile

80000hours.org/career-reviews/founding-effective-global-poverty-non-profits

High-end law (for earning to give)

Practicing law is one of the highest-earning options for someone with strong verbal skills, so could be suitable for earning to give, however, it suffers from low job satisfaction, high initial training costs, low direct impact and a potentially negative culture. We also think entering law likely narrows your options more than comparable routes. So, overall it doesn't seem like an especially promising option relative to nearby alternatives.

Studying law, however, is a common first step in a policy career, especially in the USA (though no longer in the UK). So, it may still make sense to study if you're strongly considering a career in the policy world.

Pros:

- Aids entry into high-potential policy jobs.
- Practicing law is potentially very high-earning, making it suitable for earning to give.

Cons:

- A significant fraction of lawyers are unhappy with their work, and the work has many negative features.
- It's expensive to enter this career.
- High-earning law seems very competitive, requiring extremely long hours.
- There may be some potential to make a difference directly, but high competition also suggests it's not the most promising path for this.

Career capital	Direct impact	Earnings	Advocacy potential	Ease of competition	Job satisfaction
●●●○○	●●○○○	●●●●○	●●●○○	●○○○○	●○○○○

Key facts on fit

Must be able to handle extremely long hours, work seems less interesting than alternatives, relatively strong verbal skills.

Next steps

A law degree is a relatively big commitment, so we recommend learning more about your options in policy and legal practice before making the plunge. If unsure, consider first testing out some other paths that better keep your options open.

Full profile

80000hours.org/career-reviews/high-end-law

Journalism

Journalism offers the opportunity to spread important information to a wide audience, whilst building a strong and broad network. However, the industry is shrinking, so we recommend only pursuing it whilst keeping other options open.

Pros:

- Can spread important information to a large audience and shape public debate and opinion.
- Build a strong and broad network of contacts, which is useful both for advocacy and as a backup for entry to other careers.
- Possibility of freelance work, which offers flexible hours and possibility of remote work.

Cons:

- Shrinking industry due to ongoing shift to digital journalism.
- Often takes a long time to get a paid position due to high level of competition.
- Low salaries, especially at the start of your career.
- Fast pace with constant deadlines and long hours.

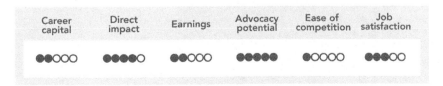

Career capital	Direct impact	Earnings	Advocacy potential	Ease of competition	Job satisfaction
●●○○○	●●●●○	●●○○○	●●●●●	●○○○○	●●●○○

Key facts on fit

Ability to write engaging stories for a big audience.

Next steps

Start writing articles for a blog and try getting pieces published in existing venues. It helps to use your network to get introductions to editors. Afterward apply very widely to jobs.

Full profile

80000hours.org/career-reviews/journalism

Management consulting (for skill-building & earning to give)

Consulting is a promising path, offering good career capital that keeps your options open and your earnings high. However, it's highly competitive and we have a limited understanding of its potential for direct impact.

Consider a job in consulting if you have strong academic credentials, aren't sure about your long-term plans and want to experience work in a variety of business environments, don't have a high impact alternative immediately available, or you want to earn to give but are not a good fit for quantitative trading or technology entrepreneurship.

Pros:

- Experience work in a wide variety of industries.
- Network with impressive colleagues.
- High earnings.

Cons:

- Highly competitive.
- Long hours.
- Limited direct impact.

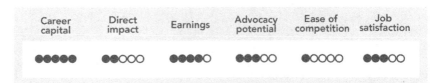

Career capital	Direct impact	Earnings	Advocacy potential	Ease of competition	Job satisfaction
●●●●●	●●○○○	●●●●○	●●●○○	●○○○○	●●●○○

Key facts on fit

Must be able to put up with 60-hour work-weeks, frequent travel, lots of PowerPoint presentations. High academic achievement a predictor, but technical knowledge not required.

Next steps

College students with a strong interest in consulting should apply for a summer internship the year before they complete their studies. It's also common to enter after graduate programs, especially MBAs. Others should meet consultants and apply if interested.

Full profile

80000hours.org/career-reviews/management-consulting

Marketing (for skill-building & earning to give)

Spending a few years doing marketing in the private sector can teach you highly generalizable skills that can later be used in a wide range of industries and causes. You should consider marketing if you have good social and verbal skills, want a decent work-life balance and want to keep your options open across causes.

Pros:

- Marketing is a valuable and highly transferable skill-set that keeps your options open across industries and causes.
- A decent chance of reaching leadership positions in companies and good preparation for entrepreneurship.
- Better work-life balance than finance, law and consulting.
- Reasonably well-paid (after a few years).

Cons:

- Some industries and marketing practices may be harmful.
- Corporate culture can reduce altruistic motivation.
- Not as prestigious or well-paid as finance, consulting, law.

Career capital	Direct impact	Earnings	Advocacy potential	Ease of competition	Job satisfaction
●●●●○	●○○○○	●●●○○	●○○○○	●●●○○	●●●○○

Key facts on fit

Ability to communicate ideas very clearly, very social and able to get on well with a wide range of people, want decent work-life balance.

Next steps

To get a sense of what's involved in marketing, you can buy and read case studies used for teaching marketing at business schools. Taking classes in business, economics or statistics can increase your chances of getting a position. The best way to get a full-time position is through internships – large consumer-product companies and some tech firms do on-campus recruitment at universities; for other industries use your network or contact firms directly.

Full profile

80000hours.org/career-reviews/work-in-marketing

Medical careers

Medicine is a highly paid and highly satisfying career. However, working in clinical medicine has a modest direct impact, and relative to the cost and time required for medical training, it has mediocre 'exit opportunities' to other career paths, and provides little platform for advocacy. It is also highly competitive.

Our view is that the people likely to succeed at medical school admission could often have a greater impact outside medicine. Within medicine, we believe the highest impact opportunities lie in the fields of (in order) biomedical research, public health and health policy, and healthcare management.

Pros:

- Generally doctors are very satisfied by their jobs, and enjoy high levels of life satisfaction and well-being.
- They are amongst the highest-paid professions, and reliably earn a high salary.
- There is reasonable variety among medical specialties, and thus the ability to select a specialty that suits one's interests, personal characteristics, or particular approach to having a large impact.

Cons:

- The direct impact of being a doctor is modest, and smaller than 'conventional wisdom' may suggest.
- Although medicine is a respected qualification, it has modest career capital for transitioning into other jobs relative to the amount of time and money it demands

(especially outside healthcare). It is also very hard to change careers in medicine after entering a training program for a given specialty.

- Similarly, although doctors enjoy widespread public esteem, they do not have a great platform for advocacy given the costs involved.

Career capital	Direct impact	Earnings	Advocacy potential	Ease of competition	Job satisfaction
●●○○○	●●●○○	●●●●○	●●●○○	●●○○○	●●●●●

Key facts on fit

Strong academic achievement, particularly in science, a caring ethos, resilience to stress and distressing situations, tolerance of long hours and unpleasant bodily fluids.

Full profile

80000hours.org/career-reviews/medical-careers

Nursing

Nurses perform a very wide range of tasks to heal the sick and keep people healthy. Nurses, especially advanced practice nurses, can earn significant amounts in some countries, permitting 'earning to give'. The entrance requirements are lower than any careers that we strongly recommend.

Nonetheless, we don't recommend nursing to many people because (i) specializing in nursing does not open up many if any options outside of medicine, (ii) it appears higher salaries are available in other non-physician medical careers, (iii) we estimate that the impact of further medical care on health in the developed world is small.

However, if nursing is particularly appealing to you, and you have already explored your other options and decided to specialize, there are opportunities to have a significant social impact by being a nurse.

Pros:

- Medium salaries in some countries, particularly the USA, and high salaries for advanced specialties.
- High meaningfulness of work.
- Relatively uncompetitive for a graduate profession, with a high likelihood of employment.

267

Cons:

- Little flexibility because the skills developed are not easily transferred outside nursing.
- Difficult work and high rate of burnout.
- Low potential for advocacy, and less prestige than medicine.

Career capital	Direct impact	Earnings	Advocacy potential	Ease of competition	Job satisfaction
●●○○○	●●●○○	●●○○○	●○○○○	●●●●●	●●●●○

Key facts on fit

Social skills and compassion, ability to deal with physical work and high pressure situations (and for advanced practice: memory and attention to detail).

Next steps

While qualifications vary by country, becoming a registered nurse will usually require a three-year undergraduate degree at a nursing school. After practicing as a nurse for a few years, you can then pursue a Master's course to become an advanced practice nurse.

Full profile

80000hours.org/career-reviews/nursing

Party politics

This is a very high-potential, though very competitive and high-risk path that can enable you to make a big difference through improving the operation of government and promoting important ideas. If you're highly able, could tolerate being in the public eye and think you could develop a strong interest in politics, then we recommend learning more about this career to test your suitability.

Pros:

- If you have aptitude for the job, then your expected influence is very large, holding the potential for a large impact if you can advance better policies than would have been promoted otherwise.

Cons:

- Chances of reaching highly influential positions are small.
- Although you can exit into other policy positions, embarking on this path seems to narrow your options more than many others.
- It's a tough job, requiring long hours and the ability to face press scrutiny.
- It may be hard to stick to your values while seeking power and needing to make political compromises.

Career capital	Direct impact	Earnings	Advocacy potential	Ease of competition	Job satisfaction
●●●○○	●●●●●	●●○○○	●●●●●	●○○○○	●●○○○

Key facts on fit

Strong social skills, ability to toe the party line and withstand press scrutiny, long hours.

Next steps

If interested, get involved with student politics or work in an MP's office with the aim of testing your suitability and learning more. You could also consider working in the civil service Fast Stream or a think tank, though these paths are less direct.

Full profile

80000hours.org/career-reviews/party-politics-uk

Philosophy PhD

Philosophy, especially some areas within ethics and political philosophy, is plausibly a high-value area for research, and, if one is successful within philosophy, may also provide a good basis for impact via being a public intellectual. However, because of the current nature of the academic job market for philosophy, and because a philosophy PhD scores poorly in terms of career capital and keeping one's options open, we currently believe that a philosophy PhD is unlikely to be the best choice for the majority of people who are considering that option. It's important to note that almost all professional philosophers who have written publicly on this topic advise against aiming to become a philosopher as a career, unless "there is nothing else you can imagine doing".

We would recommend pursuing philosophy as a career only if one has explored and rejected other career options, and only if you get into a top-twelve PhD program: Berkeley, Columbia, Harvard, MIT, Oxford, NYU, Pittsburgh, Princeton, Rutgers, Stanford, UCLA, and Yale.

Pros:

- Potential to do important research in a variety of neglected areas.
- If successful, potential to have a role as a public intellectual.
- If successful, high degree of autonomy and intellectual satisfaction.

Cons:

- Extremely competitive, and job prospects aren't certain even for PhD students from very good universities.
- The PhD takes a long time (four to eight years) to complete, and has poor general career capital.

Career capital	Direct impact	Earnings	Advocacy potential	Ease of competition	Job satisfaction
●○○○○	●●○○○	●○○○○	●●○○○	●○○○○	●●●○○

Key facts on fit

Strong interest in philosophy, strong skills in logical reasoning and clear writing, ability to spend long periods of time autonomously doing research.

Next steps

We would encourage you to explore other career options prior to pursuing a career as a philosopher. If you are committed to academia as a path, consider investing the time to retrain and enter a PhD program with better long-term prospects, such as economics.

If you wish to do a philosophy PhD, you should have a major in philosophy at undergraduate level or a Master's degree in philosophy. Doing the Oxford BPhil (if you can get in) is a particularly good opportunity for learning about whether a career as a professional philosopher is right for you.

Full profile

80000hours.org/career-reviews/philosophy-phd

Policy-oriented civil service

Working in the civil service doesn't seem the most promising place to start your career, due to apparently poorer career capital from most roles. An exception is the UK's 'Fast Stream', which provides rapid progression to management positions.

It's more promising, however, as an area to enter later in your career. We suspect that being involved in policy-setting provides substantial opportunities for a generally able, altruistic person to make a difference (although we're uncertain about the extent to which this is true, and we're keen to learn more).

Pros:

- Likely to be significant opportunities for an able, altruistic person to improve policy-making.
- Can gain access to top policy-makers and politicians.
- Shorter and more flexible hours than in the corporate sector.

Cons:

- Weaker career capital, unless you can enter the competitive 'Fast Stream'.
- Frustrations from bureaucracy and political compromise.
- Lower salaries than from corporate jobs.

Career capital	Direct impact	Earnings	Advocacy potential	Ease of competition	Job satisfaction
●●○○○	●●●●○	●●○○○	●●●●○	●●●●○	●●●○○

Key facts on fit

Well-rounded skill profile, happy to work in a very large organization, able to stick to values in the face of political compromise.

Next steps

Read the online information on policy-oriented roles provided by the UK civil service. If interested after that, we recommend testing your suitability by making a round of applications.

Full profile

80000hours.org/career-reviews/policy-oriented-civil-service-uk

274

Product manager in tech

Product management is one of the best non-programming roles in the tech industry, and tech is one of the most attractive industries to work in. It builds more widely-applicable skills than software engineering roles and has comparable pay. Programming experience isn't necessary, but it's also a great next step for software engineers.

Pros:

- Gain a wide range of valuable skills, especially the soft skills needed for senior roles that are harder to develop in technical jobs.
- Influence and responsibility early in your career.
- Relatively highly paid (comparable to software engineering but less than quantitative trading, high-end law, and management consulting).
- Programming and university-level quantitative skills not required.

Cons:

- Difficult to enter immediately from university.
- Can be stressful and involves a lot of multitasking.
- Can lose specialist skills.

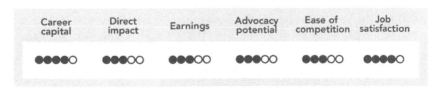

Career capital	Direct impact	Earnings	Advocacy potential	Ease of competition	Job satisfaction
●●●●○	●●●○○	●●●○○	●●●○○	●●●○○	●●●●○

Key facts on fit

Experience working in a tech company; exceptional communication and people skills (e.g. you have successfully run teams before); ability to handle many conflicting demands on your time.

Next steps

If you don't have experience, apply to a product management graduate scheme at a large company or go into software engineering or user experience design first. If you already work in tech, try moving into product management in your current company or apply for product management jobs in other companies.

Full profile

80000hours.org/career-reviews/product-manager-in-tech

Program manager in international organizations

The influence of international organizations suggests working within them is an opportunity for substantial impact if you have good personal fit for the role and are strongly motivated by social impact. However, we don't yet have a good understanding of this area.

Career capital	Direct impact	Earnings	Advocacy potential	Ease of competition	Job satisfaction
●●●○○	●●●●○	●●○○○	●●●●○	●●○○○	●●●●○

Key facts on fit
Well-rounded, expertise in relevant area.

Next steps
We recommend first learning more about these roles through internships. You'll need to build up several years of relevant experience through graduate studies or working in policy or non-profits before you can apply to paid positions.

Full profile
80000hours.org/career-reviews/program-manager-in-international-organisations

Pursuing fame in art and entertainment

While there is the potential for huge earnings, advocacy power and direct impact, the odds are stacked against even very talented individuals. A very large number of people attempt to achieve success in the arts for reasons unrelated to its social impact, making it unlikely to be a neglected area. For most people, a career in arts and entertainment is unlikely to be the path with the highest potential to do good, so we suggest you consider your other options first.

However, as with all careers, if you think you could be truly exceptional and fulfilled within this career, but not in others, you should strongly consider it.

Pros:

- High levels of job meaningfulness and autonomy.
- The possibility of obtaining very large amounts of money and social influence.

Cons:

- The field is crowded and highly competitive.
- Earnings are very unevenly distributed, making this a high-risk option, with the most likely outcome being little income or influence.
- A large amount of high-quality art already exists for people to enjoy.
- Sometimes low transferability of skills, and potentially low prestige in cases where your career doesn't take off.

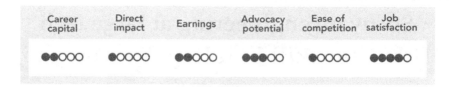

Career capital	Direct impact	Earnings	Advocacy potential	Ease of competition	Job satisfaction
●●○○○	●○○○○	●●○○○	●●●○○	●○○○○	●●●●○

Key facts on fit

Much stronger verbal/social than quantitative skills, tolerance of high risk, art is highly motivating on a day-to-day basis.

Next steps

We suggest that you seek frank feedback from masters in your art form on whether you show outstanding potential for someone at your stage in your career.

We suggest you try to reach checkpoints in your art form that indicate a higher likelihood of future success (e.g. getting into highly competitive programs such as the Iowa Writers' Workshop).

As you proceed, also aim to develop transferrable skills and contacts that will allow you to switch to other socially valuable careers if this becomes necessary.

Full profile

80000hours.org/career-reviews/pursuing-fame-in-art-and-entertainment

Software engineering at large tech firms (for skill-building & earning to give)

Software engineering at large tech-firms is a promising option that's especially easy to test out. If you have good analytical skills (even if you are from a humanities background), you should strongly consider testing it.

Pros:

- Gain a great skill-set that's in short supply, opening up a wide range of options.
- Excellent working conditions - often shorter, flexible hours, with possibility of remote work.
- In the US, the pay is relatively high, especially early in your career - $100,000+ starting salary is possible.

Cons:

- Mid- and late-stage earnings lower than in many other professional jobs.
- Less opportunity to develop non-technical soft skills.

Career capital	Direct impact	Earnings	Advocacy potential	Ease of competition	Job satisfaction
●●●●○	●●●○○	●●●○○	●●○○○	●●●○○	●●●●○

Key facts on fit

Ability to break problems down into logical parts, generate and test hypotheses, willingness to try out many different solutions, high attention to detail, quantitative degree not required.

Next steps

You can easily test your fit by trying out coding, taking an introduction to computer science class and doing a project with other people. Many people can get an entry-level job after around a year of part-time learning, or you can do a full-time twelve-week coding bootcamp, such as App Academy (appacademy.io).

Full profile

80000hours.org/career-reviews/software-engineering

Startup early employee

Being an early employee at a startup is similar to being a startup founder, except (i) the impact and financial return are usually lower (ii) the risk is lower and (iii) the personal demands are lower. It's a promising path if you'd like to found a startup, but don't have a good idea and co-founder, or want a less demanding option.

Career capital	Direct impact	Earnings	Advocacy potential	Ease of competition	Job satisfaction
●●●●○	●●●○○	●●●○○	●●○○○	●●○○○	●●●●●

Key facts on fit
A generalist who's especially independent and risk-seeking.

Next steps
The best startup jobs are found through referrals, so start by reaching out to everyone you know for leads. If that doesn't work, do something to build up your network in the technology sector for a year or two, such as software engineering at a large tech firm. You can also try Angel List (angel.co/jobs) – the largest directory of startup jobs. If you're an engineer, also try TripleByte (triplebyte.com). To find tech startups focused on important social problems, see our tips in the full profile.

Full profile
80000hours.org/career-reviews/startup-early-employee

282

Teaching

Better teachers lead to better economic outcomes, higher attendance at better universities and lower teenage birth rates for the students they teach, and the benefits talented teachers provide to society are considerably greater than what is recouped by their salary. This is the common-sense and widely-held view, though there are some dissenting voices on the impact of schooling, at least at the tertiary level.

However, we generally do not recommend teaching as the best career path to maximize your social impact: if you're working in a rich country, the impact you have as a teacher is by improving the lives of people who are almost all going to end up in the richest 15% of the world's population. Moreover, teaching is an area that is already extremely popular among the socially motivated, so it's unlikely that you'll make as big a difference on the margin within education as you could elsewhere. Further, even the most talented classroom teacher can only impact around 30 students at a time – less than is possible using other approaches.

As with all careers, if you think you could be truly exceptional within this career, but not at others, you should strongly consider it.

Pros:

- Rewarding to be interacting directly with the beneficiaries of your work.
- You may have the opportunity to advocate for important issues with your students.
- Significant vacations, which allow you to pursue other projects on the side
- If you want to become a teacher, you are relatively likely to be able to do so, since there are so many teaching positions available.
- If you are an outstanding teacher, you may get the opportunity to teach the next generation of your country's leaders, a group that it is very important have good values and strong skills.

Cons:

- If working in a rich country, your direct impact accrues to people who are among the richest in the world.
- It's perhaps the most common path for socially motivated people to pursue, so it's harder to make a big difference within it.
- Weaker than other paths at building general-purpose skills that are in demand in other fields.
- Salaries are low for the level of skill and commitment required to be a good teacher.

Career capital	Direct impact	Earnings	Advocacy potential	Ease of competition	Job satisfaction
●○○○○	●●●○○	●●○○○	●●○○○	●●●●●	●●●●○

Key facts on fit

Must be happy with constant social interaction, able to maintain control of the classroom, a positive disposition.

Next steps

If you want to enter teaching, we'd recommend applying to Teach First in the UK, or Teach for America in the USA. These organizations enable you to get a taste for teaching over two years in a demanding position, while at the same time making you an attractive candidate for other careers in case you decide to move to a different career area. (We would rate these programs as providing 3/5 for 'career capital', rather than standard teaching's 1/5.)

Full profile

80000hours.org/career-reviews/teaching

Tech startup founder

Technology entrepreneurship is a very high-potential path, offering good career capital, with a chance of both high earnings and large direct impact. Overall, we think more people should try this path. However, it's also one of the most difficult paths, and only suits a relatively small number of people. Consider this career if you think you can develop strong technical skills, as well as the ability to deal with high risk of failure, work very long hours and do something unconventional.

Career capital	Direct impact	Earnings	Advocacy potential	Ease of competition	Job satisfaction
●●●●○	●●●●○	●●●●●	●●●○○	●○○○○	●●●●○

Key facts on fit
Intelligent, risk-taking, able to work very long hours for three to seven years, high grit, independent, can develop strong technical skills.

Next steps
If interested, we recommend you prioritize testing your potential in this path while keeping your options open. This can be done by meeting entrepreneurs, reading more, learning about important problems, and learning technical skills such as programming. After that, the normal path is to find a co-founder, build a prototype product and apply to enter a 'seed accelerator'.

Full profile

80000hours.org/career-reviews/tech-entrepreneurship

Think tank research

Working in a think tank for a few years early in your career is a plausible way to influence government policy for the better, and in the meantime gain skills and contacts to advance your future career in politics or elsewhere, while doing work that's often fulfilling.

Those with either great skills in quantitative analysis, or the ability to synthesize and communicate ideas clearly, should think carefully about how well it compares relative to their other opportunities, such as joining party politics.

Pros:

- Your colleagues are likely to be intelligent, desire to improve the world, and have similar interests to you.
- You have the potential to advocate for important issues that are neglected elsewhere.
- You gain contacts in policy and an understanding of how the public policy ecosystem can be shifted.

Cons:

- Early on in your career it may be hard to find a think tank which will hire you and also matches your personal values.
- The number of think tank research projects on the most important, neglected and tractable problems directly is relatively small.
- It is likely you will work for significant periods of time, and potentially your entire career, without successfully influencing government policy.

Career capital	Direct impact	Earnings	Advocacy potential	Ease of competition	Job satisfaction
●●●○○	●●●●○	●●○○○	●●●○○	●●○○○	●●●●○

Key facts on fit

Either good quantitative research or writing skills depending on the role; ability to synthesize and clearly communicate your and other people's research; personal interest in some area of government policy.

Next steps

Attend events put on by think tanks, network, discuss their work and get to know the people. Try to get on their radar by writing things that impress them. Being a Research Assistant is very relevant work experience. Some think tanks hire undergraduates as interns, and that is a great opportunity to see if it's a career in which you could excel. Read their reports and try to find a few that fit your temperament and beliefs.

If you are choosing your degree, the majors they hire from are wide-ranging depending on their field of interest, but often include economics, government, social sciences, law or further degrees in international relations.

Think tanks publish lists of vacancies on their websites.

Full profile

80000hours.org/career-reviews/think-tank-research

Trading in quantitative hedge funds (for earning to give)

For someone with strong quantitative skills, we think this represents one of the best career opportunities available. The pay is exceptionally good enabling earning to give, you can develop technical skills valued in academia or technology, and the work is satisfying. We've seen numerous cases of mathematicians taking this path and being highly satisfied. The main caveat is that the industry faces many risks – these activities could become unprofitable due to regulation or competition – so it's important to make sure you also build strong career capital.

Pros:

- Exceptionally high pay.
- Engaging work.
- Build skills in statistics, programming and modelling, as well as general skills like team work and decision-making under pressure.

Cons:

- Only possible to enter with very strong mathematical skills.
- Industry faces numerous risks.
- The career capital you gain is less flexible than working in the tech industry (in particular, you'll gain fewer connections).

Career capital	Direct impact	Earnings	Advocacy potential	Ease of competition	Job satisfaction
●●●○○	●○○○○	●●●●●	●●●○○	●○○○○	●●●●○

Key facts on fit

Strong mathematical skills.

Next steps

If interested, make applications to internships to try the path out – these are a quick and well-paid way to test the career.[82] We particularly recommend Jane Street (janestreet.com) due to its fast growth, high pay and good culture.

Some of these jobs are open to undergraduates, but many only accept people with PhDs.

Full profile

80000hours.org/career-reviews/trading-in-quantitative-hedge-funds

---

[82] See lists of firms to apply to at streetofwalls.com/finance-training-courses/quantitative-hedge-fund-training/quant-firms and quora.com/What-are-the-best-quant-hedge-funds.

Valuable academic research

The potential of academic research is very sensitive to your degree of personal fit. If you're an unusually good fit for a high-priority field of study, then it's a very strong option. However, we think it's common for people to continue with academic research when they'd be better suited elsewhere, so we encourage you to be self-skeptical and test out other options.

Pros:

- If you're a good fit, you have the potential to have a large direct impact.
- An academic position can give you a good public platform for advocacy.

Cons:

- Competitive 'up or out' progression with high drop-out rates in most fields.
- Need to 'publish or perish' and teaching requirements make it harder to work on satisfying, high impact projects, especially early in your career.

Career capital	Direct impact	Earnings	Advocacy potential	Ease of competition	Job satisfaction
●●●○○	●●●●○	●●○○○	●●●●○	●○○○○	●●●●○

Key facts on fit

Intelligent, high grit, autonomous, deep interest in area.

Next steps

If you're unsure whether academic research is for you, then continue studying, while looking to try out other options in your holidays and in the years between undergraduate and graduate study. It can be hard to re-enter academia (especially after a PhD) so this better keeps your options open.

Note that we have separate specific profiles for biomedical research, Economics PhD and Computer Science PhD.

Full profile

80000hours.org/career-reviews/valuable-academic-research

Web designer

Web designers create the look and layout of web pages. Their skills are in demand in many types of organizations, from charities to startups, giving you flexibility to work on high impact projects. As a backup, you can enter paths with good pay, like UX design ($80k median salary), and earn to give. However, good design is hard to measure, which makes it hard to prove your abilities to potential employers, meaning entry and progression can be difficult. You should consider web design if you studied graphic design or a related field, you've already spent several years developing good taste in web design, and you have strong persuasion skills that enable you to get a foot in the door when you're starting out. However, if you have the technical skills to do web development, we recommend you do that instead, since it has higher pay, more jobs, and entry and progression is easier.

Pros:

- Useful skill-set that can be used to work directly on a wide range of important problems.
- Freelance and remote work widely available.
- Good outlook (similar to web developers).
- Less competitive and uses more visual skill than our other recommended paths.
- Fall back option to earn to give by transitioning into higher-paid UX design (median salary ~$80,000).

Cons:

- Entry and progression can be difficult because good design is hard to measure.
- Salaries, number of jobs and job growth rate lower than in web development, so if that's open to you, consider going into web development.

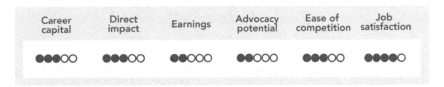

Career capital	Direct impact	Earnings	Advocacy potential	Ease of competition	Job satisfaction
●●●○○	●●●○○	●●○○○	●●○○○	●●●○○	●●●●○

Key facts on fit

Visual arts background, well-developed taste in web design informed by feedback from other designers, strong communication skills, good at persuasion and negotiation.

Next steps

1. Learn basic design skills. The best online resource we found is HackDesign (hackdesign.org/lessons).
2. Build a portfolio.
3. Apply widely to jobs.

Full profile

80000hours.org/career-reviews/web-designer

APPENDIX 9

Problem profile summaries

As part of our research, we've evaluated different problem areas. We drew on work by other groups to assess them on scale, neglectedness and solvability - a framework we introduced earlier in the guide.[83] We also tried to find the most effective ways people can contribute to solving these problems in their careers.

We've included summaries of these problem profiles below, but we're always updating them. So to see the full and most up-to-date versions of the profiles, please go to:

http://80k.link/VEK

---

[83] To learn more about how we made the assessment, see 80000hours.org/articles/problem-framework.

Biosecurity

Natural pandemics and new scientifically engineered pathogens could potentially kill millions or even billions of people. Future progress in synthetic biology is likely to increase the risk and severity of pandemics from engineered pathogens. There are promising paths to reducing these risks through regulating potentially dangerous research, improving early detection systems and developing better international emergency response plans.

Factor	Score	Notes
Scale	12/14	Outbreaks of engineered pathogens could cause a global catastrophe
Neglectedness	6/11	Over $1 billion spent by US government.
Solvability	4/5	Some plausible ways to make progress, with some expert support

How to contribute to tackling this problem

Options for working on this problem include working at foundations focused on biosecurity (Open Philanthropy Project, Gates Foundation and Skoll Global Threats Fund), working for the US government (Centers for Disease Control and Prevention, and National Institutes of Health), and doing a

PhD and working at synthetic biology labs to gain expertise in the area and promote a culture of safety.

Full profile

80000hours.org/problem-profiles/biosecurity

Climate change (extreme risks)

According to current estimates, unmitigated greenhouse emissions are likely to lead to global temperature increases of 2.6ºC to 4.8ºC by 2100. If this happened, there'd likely be significant humanitarian harms, including more severe weather, food crises, and the spread of infectious diseases which would disproportionately affect the world's worst off.

But there is a non-negligible chance that unmitigated emissions will lead to *even larger* increases in global temperatures, the results of which could be catastrophic for life on Earth. Though the chance of such large increases is relatively low, the degree of harm that would result is very high, meaning that the expected value of working to reduce these extreme risks may also be very high.

You are more likely to think that extreme climate change is among the most pressing global problems if you think that we have obligations to people who do not yet exist and that there is great value in ensuring that human civilization continues in the long-term.

Factor	Score	Notes
Scale	13/14	Extreme climate change could have catastrophic consequences for human civilization.
Neglectedness	3/11	The resources dedicated to preventing climate change globally, including both inside and outside all governments, are probably $100-1,000 billion per year. However, we are downgrading that to an effective $10-100 billion per year, because much of this spending (i) would have happened for other reasons, (ii) is not focused on the extreme risks of climate change, (iii) is poorly allocated.
Solvability	4/5	Coordination is difficult due to the free-rider problem. However, some options such as efficiency are straightforward.

How to contribute to tackling this problem

Options for working on this problem include academic research into the extreme risks of climate change or whether they might be mitigated by geoengineering. One can also advocate for reduced greenhouse emissions through careers in politics, think tanks or journalism, and work on developing emissions-lowering technologies as an engineer or scientist.

Full profile

80000hours.org/problem-profiles/climate-change

Factory farming

Each year, 50 billion animals are raised and slaughtered in factory farms globally. Over a billion animals live in factory farms at any point of time in the United States. Most experience serious levels of suffering. The problem is neglected relative to its scale – less than $20 million per year is spent trying to solve it.

There are promising paths to improving the conditions of factory-farmed animals and for changing attitudes towards farm animals.

Note on scope: These scores are for attempts to make people in the United States care enough about animals to become vegetarian or vegan.

Factor	Score	Notes
Scale	11/14	We think intense efforts to reduce meat consumption could reduce factory farming in the US by 10-90% and contribute to spreading more humane values.
Neglectedness	8/11	Between $10 and 100 million in annual funding; 1,000 people working on the problem.

Solvability	4/5	Some plausible ways to make progress, with some expert support.

How to contribute to tackling this problem

Options for working on this problem include: supporting the organizations recommended by Animal Charity Evaluators[84] by taking a high-earning job and donating to them or by working at them directly; working at companies developing plant-based alternatives to meat; and advocating for action on the problem as an academic, journalist or politician.

Full profile

80000hours.org/problem-profiles/factory-farming

---

[84] See animalcharityevaluators.org/recommendations/top-charities.

Global priorities research

Every year governments, foundations and individuals spend over $500 billion on efforts to improve the world as a whole. This isn't enough money to solve all the world's problems, and so difficult decisions have to be made about which global problems to prioritize.

Recent research has found that there are large differences in effectiveness between different approaches to improving the world. But of the $500 billion spent each year, only a miniscule fraction (less than 0.01%) is spent on global priorities research: efforts to work out which global problems are the most pressing to work on (e.g. climate change vs poverty vs education). With a track record of already influencing hundreds of millions of dollars, future research could lead to billions of dollars being spent many times more effectively.

Based on our analysis, we believe this is one of the highest impact fields you can work in.

Factor	Score	Notes
Scale	11/14	It seems plausible that better prioritization within international organizations, governments and charities could do more than save 10 million years of life (through redirecting over a billion dollars to highly effective health interventions). Or that

		better understanding of existential risk reduction priorities could lower extinction risk by between 0.01% and 0.1%. However, there's a lot of uncertainty about how much better research would be adopted.
Neglectedness	11/11	Spending in the main global prioritization groups is between $1 and 10 million a year.
Solvability	3/5	Significant uncertainty about how to approach, solution at least a decade off.

How to contribute to tackling this problem

Options for working on this problem including taking a researcher, manager or support role at one of the following or donating a percentage of your income to fund their research:

- The Open Philanthropy Project (www.openphilanthropy.org),
- The Global Priorities Project (globalprioritiesproject.org), or
- The Future of Humanity Institute (www.fhi.ox.ac.uk).

Alternatively you could pursue a PhD in economics, math, statistics or social science and undertake relevant research in academia. Or you could work in governments or foundations and influence spending based on the latest results of global priorities research.

Full profile

80000hours.org/problem-profiles/global-priorities-research

Health in poor countries

Every year around ten million people in poorer countries die of illnesses that can be very cheaply prevented or managed, including malaria, HIV, tuberculosis and diarrhea.

Around $100 per capita is spent on the healthcare of the poorest 2 billion people each year (adjusted for purchasing power parity). As a result there remain many opportunities to scale-up treatments that are known to prevent or cure these conditions.

Factor	Score	Notes
Scale	13/14	The damage done by easily-preventable diseases in the least developed countries plus India is between 200 million and 500 million DALYs per year.
Neglectedness	2/11	The least developed countries plus India spend about $300 billion on health each year (PPP).
Solvability	5/5	The problem is mostly a matter of scaling up approaches that are known, with near certainty to work if done correctly.

How to contribute to tackling this problem

Options for working on the problem include as a donor to effective projects, as an economist in intergovernmental organizations such as the World Bank or World Health Organization, or by starting or working in a non-profit that scales up proven treatments.

Full profile

80000hours.org/problem-profiles/health-in-poor-countries

Land use reform

Local laws often prohibit the construction of dense new housing, which drives up prices, especially in a few large high-wage urban areas. The increased prices transfer wealth from renters to landowners and push people away from centers of economic activity, which reduces their ability to get jobs or earn higher wages, likely by a very large amount.

The direct beneficiaries of progress on this problem would mostly be middle-class people in developed countries – not the most needy of groups globally. However, if you believe economic growth, wage increases and technological advancement in developed countries are valuable goals, this is one of the more promising policy changes for raising productivity.

Factor	Score	Notes
Scale	10/14	The gain in economic output has been estimated to be in the ballpark of $100 billion.
Neglectedness	7/11	While impossible to get hard figures on, we think given the enormous profit opportunities, at least $100 million is likely spent each year on attempts to allow more construction in these key US cities. This estimate is uncertain.

Solvability	3/5	There is both strong established opposition and significant expert support behind policy change in this area.

How to contribute to tackling this problem

An opportunity to tackle the problem which nobody has yet taken is to start a non-profit or lobbying body to advocate for more housing construction in key urban areas and states. Another option would be to try to shift zoning decisions from local to state governments, where they are less likely to be determined by narrow local interests, especially existing landowners who benefit from higher property prices.

Full profile

80000hours.org/problem-profiles/land-use-reform

Nuclear security

Nuclear weapons that are armed at all times have the potential to kill hundreds of millions of people directly, and billions due to subsequent effects on agriculture. They pose some unknown risk of human extinction through the potential for a 'nuclear winter' and a social collapse from which we never recover. There are many examples in history of moments in which the US or Russia came close to accidentally or deliberately using their nuclear weapons.

Nuclear security is already a major topic of interest for governments, making it harder to have an effect on the situation.

Factor	Score	Notes
Scale	14/14	Nuclear war would have devastating impacts.
Neglectedness	5/11	$1 to 10b of annual spending.
Solvability	3/5	Some possible ways to make progress, with significant controversy.

How to contribute to tackling this problem

Most opportunities to influence the risk from nuclear weapons seem to be through work in the military or foreign policy establishments, or research in the think tanks that offer them ideas for how to lower the risk of nuclear conflict. Some less conventional approaches would be working independently to improve relationships between people in the nuclear powers, or trying to improve the resilience of our food supply in the case of a serious agricultural collapse.

Full profile

80000hours.org/problem-profiles/nuclear-security

Promoting effective altruism

Effective altruism is a growing social movement that applies evidence and reason to find the most effective ways to help others. Promoting its ideas can increase your impact many times over, through influencing other altruists to pursue the very best opportunities for doing good. Past efforts to promote effective altruism have already caused more than 2,000 people to pledge to donate at least 10% of their income to highly effective charities, with three-quarters of a billion dollars in pledged lifetime donations. Promoting effective altruism also builds a community that will work on whichever problems turn out to be most pressing in the future, so it's a good option if you're unsure about which problem is most pressing.

Factor	Score	Notes
Scale	13/14	We think it's plausible that the effective altruism movement, once at full maturity, could save 100-1,000 million years of live a year, by causing $10-100 billion a year to be spent on much more effective projects. This estimate is necessarily highly uncertain.

Neglectedness	10/11	The annual budget of all money focused on promoting effective altruism is less than US$10m and will probably remain that way for the next few years. However one might think other kinds of spending already promote the ideas of effective altruism to some extent, e.g. promotion of evidence based policy. As a result we are estimating the resources spent as $10-100m.
Solvability	3.5/5	Some natural support among relevant people, but some opposition.

How to contribute to tackling this problem

If you're new, the best thing is to get involved with the effective altruism community. More information is available at Chapter 9 of this book. You can also:

- Apply for an internship or job at an effective altruist organization or projects.
- Start or join an effective altruism local group, which will give you experience in talking about effective altruism, and which is a good way to build up credentials for working at an effective altruism organization, as well as having a direct impact.
- Promote effective altruism via journalism, politics, academia or even just social media. Building up an

audience gives you the ability to advocate for important ideas.

Full profile

80000hours.org/problem-profiles/promoting-effective-altruism

Risks posed by artificial intelligence

Many experts believe that there is a significant chance we'll create artificially intelligent machines with abilities surpassing those of humans – superintelligence – sometime during this century. These advances could lead to extremely positive developments, but could also pose risks due to catastrophic accidents or misuse. The people working on this problem aim to maximize the chance of a positive outcome, while reducing the chance of catastrophe.

Work on the risks posed by superintelligent machines seems largely neglected, with total funding for this research well under $10 million a year.

Factor	Score	Notes
Scale	14/14	We estimate that the risk of extinction from AI within the next 200 years is in the order of 10%, and that a research program on the topic could reduce that by at least one percentage point. These estimates are necessarily highly uncertain.
Neglectedness	11/11	$1 to 10m of annual funding.

Solvability	2/5	Solutions are believed to be several decades off and it is quite unclear how to approach the problem. Some dispute whether it is possible to address the problem today.

How to work on this problem

The primary opportunity to deal with the problem is to conduct research in philosophy, computer science and mathematics aimed at keeping an AI's actions and goals in alignment with human intentions, even if it were much more capable than humans at all tasks. There are also indirect ways of approaching the problem, such as increasing the number of people worried about the risks posed by artificial intelligence and their capability to act in the future.

Full profile

80000hours.org/problem-profiles/artificial-intelligence-risk

Smoking in the developing world

Smoking takes an enormous toll on human health – accounting for about 6% of all ill-health globally according to the best estimates. This is more than HIV and malaria combined. Despite this, smoking is on the rise in many developing countries as people become richer and can afford to buy cigarettes.

Factor	Score	Notes
Scale	11/14	The damage done by smoking in developing countries is around 100 million years of healthy life annually, and this could plausibly be halved.
Neglectedness	7/11	The collective value of philanthropy and bureaucrats working on tobacco control is between $100 and $1,000 million.
Solvability	3/5	Some relevant people are supportive but there's significant opposition from the status quo.

How to contribute to tackling this problem

There appears to be a range of policies which have been shown to reduce smoking rates, which are usually not applied in developing countries. The most natural ways to tackle the problem through your career include becoming a health policy expert, or advocacy through journalism, think tanks and politics. This is a particularly promising area for people living in a developing country with high smoking rates.

Full profile

80000hours.org/problem-profiles/tobacco

Further reading

Books

Flourish, by Prof. Martin Seligman, is a survey of the findings of positive psychology from the last couple of decades, by the founder of the field. A bit rambly (compared to his excellent earlier work), but full of fascinating ideas and examples.

Stumbling Upon Happiness, by Prof. Dan Gilbert, outlines the science of measuring happiness, and explains why we're so bad at judging what will make us happy.

Give and Take, by Prof. Adam Grant, outlines the evidence that having an altruistic mindset can make you more successful, so long as you avoid burnout. It then goes on to explain how you can avoid burnout.

Altruism, by Matthieu Ricard, makes a detailed argument that it's best both for yourself and the world if you focus on helping others.

Doing Good Better, Will MacAskill (co-founder of 80,000 Hours), an introduction to effective altruism.

How to Spend $75 Billion to Make the World a Better Place, by Bjorn Lomborg, based on the research of the Copenhagen

Consensus, which asks leading economists to prioritize among different ways to help the global poor.

Superintelligence, by Nick Bostrom, the key book about the risks of artificial intelligence.

So Good They Can't Ignore You, by Cal Newport (a fan of 80,000 hours), which argues you should focus on building career capital rather than following your passion if you want to have a good career.

The Startup of You, by Reid Hoffman the founder of LinkedIn, which presents a new approach to career planning based on exploration and flexibility. It also contains great tips on networking.

What Color is Your Parachute, by Dick Bolles, the bestselling career advice book of all time. You can get an overview of the basics of job hunting here.

Getting Past No, by William Ury of Harvard Law School's Program on Negotiation, is a classic guide to how to negotiate.

Essays and resources

Famine, Affluence and Morality, by Peter Singer, the classic essay making the moral argument for focusing on helping others with most of your time and money:
philosophyfaculty.ucsd.edu/faculty/rarneson/Singeressaysp ring1972.pdf

Giving without sacrifice, by Andreas Mogensen, which explores whether giving 10% of your income to charity will make you happier:
www.givingwhatwecan.org/sites/givingwhatwecan.org/files/attachments/giving-without-sacrifice.pdf

Speciesism and moral status, by Peter Singer, an argument for the moral value of animals:
www.oswego.edu/~delancey/Singer.pdf

More detail on the argument for focusing on international development rather than developed country poverty:
www.givewell.org/giving101/Your-dollar-goes-further-overseas

The concept of existential risk, and what it means for choosing which problem to work on:
www.existential-risk.org/concept.html

The pre-interview project:
https://medium.com/life-learning/how-to-get-any-job-you-want-even-if-you-re-unqualified-6f49a65f5491

How to negotiate your salary:
http://www.kalzumeus.com/2012/01/23/salary-negotiation/

How to network:
80000hours.org/2015/03/how-to-network/

See how rich you are compared to everyone else:
www.givingwhatwecan.org/get-involved/how-rich-am-i/

You read everything? Here's what's next

If you're looking to plan out your next career move, try out our career planning tool:
http://80k.link/HWC

If you've already got a plan, one of the most powerful things you can do to have more impact is to meet others doing the same. There are thousands of people in our community helping each other succeed. To take part, have a look here:
http://80k.link/QNB

If you'd like more reading after that (we admire your stamina!), please see a list of everything on our website:
http://80k.link/VOF

If you've found this guide useful, and know someone else in the midst of planning their career, we've created a simple tool to let you deliver a copy of this guide to them:
80000hours.org/gift

Or, if you'd like to share the guide more broadly, you can do so here:
80000hours.org/shar

Acknowledgements

This book would not have been possible without help from a huge number of people, including the following:

My partner Leo, for putting up with me talking about 80,000 Hours all the time, and supporting me the last four years.

Our co-founder, Will MacAskill – without him the organization probably wouldn't exist.

Our trustees, Toby Ord and Nick Beckstead.

All the staff at 80,000 Hours – currently Robert Wiblin, Roman Duda, Peter McIntyre, Jesse Avshalomov, and Peter Hartree. In particular, we'd like to thank Maria Gutierrez and Peter Orr for their work editing and designing the book.

Everyone who has worked at 80,000 Hours in the past, including: Richard Batty, Matt Gibb, Robbie Shade, Niel Bowerman, Tom Rowlands, Seb Farquhar, Jess Whittlestone, Ozzie Gooen, Jen Brennan, Ilan Fischer, Jake Nebel, Isaac Lewis, Jeff Pole, Amber Morgan, and Kyle Scott.

Alex Mayyasi from Priceonomics, who was a great help editing the online version of many of the articles.

All of our donors, including Luke Ding, Sam Bankman-Fried, Fred Mulder, Patrick Brinich-Langlois, Jeff Kaufman, Julia Wise, Jaan Tallinn, Brian and Shauna Lonergan, Alex Gordon-Brown and Denise Melchin, Prof. Tony Purnell, and the Van Houten Fund.

All our users, who have provided us with feedback, and filled out our many surveys.

Everyone who has supported and worked at the Centre for Effective Altruism, especially those who provided our operations, including Tara MacAuley, Amy Wiley Labenz, Michelle Hutchinson, Tom Ash, George McGowan, Tonja Wright, Marek Duda and Kandasai Griffiths, and those who got the organization going in the early days, such as Holly Morgan and Matt Wage.

All the companies who have provided us with discounted services, especially Google, Search Star, and Roberts Immigration.

Everyone who has given us advice, including the staff at Y Combinator, Holden Karnofsky, Jake Gibson, Adam O'Boyle, Cal Newport, Matt Clifford, Soushiant Zanganehpour, Jeff Kaufmann, Alex Flint, all the people we've interviewed as part of our research, and many others.

We're deeply grateful.

Index

Made in the USA
Las Vegas, NV
29 April 2022

48166422R00193